Midwest Living®
SMALL-TOWN GETAWAYS
UPDATED

MIDWEST LIVING Small-Town Getaways
Project Editors: Barbara Humeston, Barbara Morrow
Assistant Editor: Ira Lacher
Contributing Editor: Benjamin Allen
Associate Art Director: Tom Wegner
Map Illustrator: Mike Burns
Production Manager: Douglas M. Johnston

MIDWEST LIVING Magazine
Editor: Dan Kaercher
Managing Editor: Barbara Humeston
Art Director: Richard Michels

Meredith Publishing Group
President: Christopher M. Little
Vice President, Consumer Marketing & Development: Hal Oringer

Meredith Corporation
Chairman and Chief Executive Officer: William T. Kerr
Chairman: E. T. Meredith III

Cover: Granville, Ohio *(see page 114)*
Photograph: Tony Walsh

There's something almost magical about Midwest small towns. Trees still meet across the streets in these communities that have refused to bow to time. Handsome courthouses, and gazebos and bandstands trimmed with architectural curlicues decorate the squares. Home-cooking cafes entice you inside with the welcoming sounds of conversation and aromas that you remember from Grandma's kitchen.

With the help of this book, small towns don't have to remain strictly places in your heart. You can visit 75 of our favorites when you're traveling around the Midwest.

We'll tell you about the towns' best sites and attractions; where you'll want to shop, eat and stay; and how the towns came to be. These are the kinds of communities where many of us grew up, surrounded by freedom and friendliness, security and sociability. They're also where many more of you have told us you still long to be.

Stop by any of these small towns for a few hours, a day or a weekend. We think you'll want to stay. And we're sure that when you steal one last glance backwards as you leave town, you'll take home some fond memories.

We would love to hear your comments about our small-town guide. Write to us at: Small Town Getaways, MIDWEST LIVING®, 1716 Locust St., Des Moines, IA 50309-3023.

Safe and happy traveling!

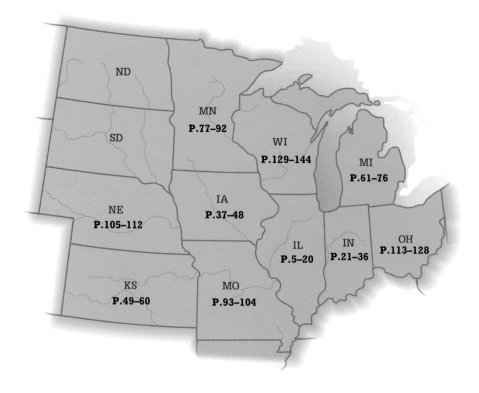

ND

MN
P.77–92

SD

WI
P.129–144

MI
P.61–76

NE
P.105–112

IA
P.37–48

IL
P.5–20

IN
P.21–36

OH
P.113–128

KS
P.49–60

MO
P.93–104

Galena

Shipshewana

Pella

Lindsborg

Frankenmuth

Lanesboro

Ste. Genevieve

Nebraska City

Yellow Springs

Fish Creek

ILLINOIS

ARTHUR/ARCOLA • ELSAH • GALENA GENESEO • GENEVA • LEBANON MAEYSTOWN • NAUVOO • PETERSBURG

● Galena
ROCKFORD ●
Geneva ●
CHICAGO ●
● Geneseo
● **PEORIA**
● Nauvoo
Petersburg ●
SPRINGFIELD ★   Arthur ● ● Arcola
● Elsah
● Lebanon
● Maeystown

From the rugged foothills of the Ozark Mountains to historic steamboat country, from big-city suburbs to peaceful rural landscapes where Abraham Lincoln's ghost still casts a long shadow, each one of these inviting communities tells its own proud story.

For information about additional Illinois small towns you can visit, contact: *Illinois Travel Center (800/2-CONNECT; TTY 800/406-6418).*

NAUVOO

Beside the Mississippi, this historic town honors its Mormon heritage and wine-making tradition.

In 1839, Joseph Smith and his Mormon followers platted Nauvoo at a sweeping horseshoe bend in the Mississippi River. In old Hebrew, the town's fitting name means "beautiful place."

The Mormons brought that vision to life in Nauvoo. Within a few years, a marble temple commanded the hill overlooking the river, and more than 2,000 buildings rose on the flats and climbed the bluffs.

The assassination of Smith and the burning of the temple forced those original settlers to flee. But their spirit lingers in Old Nauvoo, where church members restored and now tend more than 2 dozen of the original ruddy brick structures.

Volunteers dress as the first settlers might have: floor-length skirts for women, and white shirts and bow ties for men. These interpreters lead tours of the old shops and homes, and cheerfully answer questions.

Overlooking the historic area and the river, modern Nauvoo welcomes visitors and serves area farmers. You can have dinner at the 1840 Hotel Nauvoo and tour Illinois' oldest winery nearby.

Uptown Nauvoo

Modern Nauvoo grew up around the remnants of the destroyed Mormon temple. A monument and blooming gardens now mark the site.

At the white frame Hotel Nauvoo, built as a home in 1840, visitors and residents alike feast on specialties such as crunchy fried chicken in seven main-floor dining rooms. You also can stay in simple guest rooms upstairs or in one of several other bed and breakfasts in the area.

Five antiques shops and a handful of specialty stores scatter around the small downtown area. Across the street from the hotel, the Art Needle Shop specializes in Swedish embroidery. You can buy finished works or supplies to create your own.

The Nauvoo Mill and Bakery grinds wheat and corn into flour and meal. Buy a sack to take home or a loaf of freshly baked bread. At the Fudge Factory, candy-makers mold huge dollops of gooey chocolate into sweet slabs, cut into neat squares.

The Allyn House woodworking shop crafts historically accurate windows and doors for buildings at Old Nauvoo and other historic sites, including the Mark Twain home across the river in Hannibal, Missouri. Displays illustrate the methods that builders used when they worked without nails or glue. The shop also sells handcrafted wooden toys, butter churns and buckets. Some days, you might find crafter Judy Jones at work at her wheel in Nauvoo Pottery.

At Nauvoo Glassworks, visitors watch as artisans turn glistening bubbles of molten glass into delicate vases, Christmas ornaments, wineglasses and other creations.

Yesterday Lives On

Buildings of weathered, reddish orange brick rise on the grassy grounds of historic Old Nauvoo, surrounded on three sides by the Mississippi River. Some of the 150-year-old homes, shops and meeting halls stand within a few steps of the Mississippi's marshy Illinois riverbank. The structures are so close to the water, you can peer from their windows and watch dragonflies dart among the cattails.

Nauvoo's founders planned well. The great flood of 1993 and other deluges bypassed this old town. The river is broad enough along this stretch to contain even a flood, and the bend weakens the water's force.

You can walk among the buildings scattered in the shade of massive oaks and maples. Or catch a ride on the horse-drawn wagon that ferries visitors around the historic district.

Stops around the village include the 1842 home of Jonathan Browning, inventor of the repeating rifle. There, you'll see his gun collection. The aroma of freshly baked bread wafts

The best of
Nauvoo fare:
wine, blue cheese
and the Hotel
Nauvoo's crunchy
fried chicken.

from the Scovall Bakery next door.

In the general store, the shopkeeper shows young visitors a child-size antique yoke that a youngster might have used to carry buckets of water. No one can guess what it is.

"Water didn't come out of a faucet," the shopkeeper explains to the puzzled group. "Your mother would have sent you to fetch it."

You'll probably find the blacksmith bent over his forge, heating iron to make horseshoes or to repair a farm tool. In a restored brick house, visitors can view the cramped upstairs quarters where a Mormon family's children slept and the small room that served as the village school long ago.

Tragedy Strikes

The Latter Day Saints Visitors Center, an imposing contemporary structure, towers over the parklike grounds of Old Nauvoo. A film in the center's auditorium tells about the town's beginnings and the restoration that started more than 3 decades ago. You can walk through the adjacent Monument to Women sculpture garden, with its 13 graceful life-size female statues.

The Mormons built their town on fertile ground that the Sac and Fox tribes had farmed. Nauvoo was poised to boom and, for a time, the village prospered. Within 3 years, it was one of the largest communities in the state and the nation. The Mormons' sturdy brick homes and the imposing temple were the envy of the area's residents.

Yet, for all their planning, the Mormons hadn't predicted the resentment their religion and prosperity would spawn among other settlers. In 1844, Smith and his brother were assassinated in nearby Carthage, Illinois, and his followers abandoned Nauvoo. The temple burned in 1846 and, shortly thereafter, thriving Nauvoo became a ghost town.

Just 3 years later, a French communal society known as the Icarians bought the Mormon property. That settlement was short-lived, but the Icar-

The 1840s come to life in the Mormons' Old Nauvoo.

PRINTING OFFICE

POST OFF

RUSS MUNN

ians realized that the area's climate and soil matched France's best wine-making regions.

Soon, more than 600 acres of vineyards striped the area's farmlands, and stone-arched wine cellars honeycombed the surrounding hills. In the 1930s, residents found the caves ideal for aging blue cheese. The Nauvoo Cheese Company continues to produce the distinctive cheese, which a number of the town's shops sell.

The Icarian Living History Museum, in a restored century-old home along Parley Street in Nauvoo's modern section, tells the story of those settlers.

Wine-Making Tradition

Some of the area's early French immigrants planted grapes on the hill that rises just south of Old Nauvoo, now part of Nauvoo State Park. Those vines still produce grapes, and the settlers' eight-room home and winery have been preserved as a museum. The state park also provides shady picnic spots, along with good camping areas.

Emile Baxter arrived in Nauvoo in 1855 and planted grapevines. Two years later, he started making wine. Baxter's great-great-grandson, Kelly Logan, and Kelly's wife, Brenda, now oversee Baxter's Vineyards. Their winery, the state's oldest, produces more than 1,200 bottles a year.

On Labor Day weekend, Nauvoo and Baxter's Vineyards celebrate this wine-making tradition with a 3-day Grape Festival. A pageant depicts Nauvoo's history, and the event concludes with a lighthearted ceremonial wedding of the wine and cheese.

You can tour Baxter's barnlike bottling operation. In the big tasting room and gift shop, sample the varieties the winery produces. Most visitors want to try Baxter's signature vintage, a Concord grape dessert wine.

"People seem to like it," Brenda says with a chuckle, as she hands out samples. "We sure go through a lot."

By George Hendrix.

GENEVA

Shopping, historic homes and Scandinavian heritage bring visitors to this Fox River Valley town.

Just beyond the outskirts of Chicago's western suburbs, the Fox River meanders through a broad valley. Even though the Midwest's largest city is merely an hour's drive east, woods and farmland still dominate much of this peaceful countryside.

Forests once flanked the river from its source near the Illinois-Wisconsin state line. Loggers felled mountains of timber, and sawmills rose on the river's banks. The mills attracted workers and other businesses, and towns grew up around them.

While some of the river towns attracted this new brawny industry, the village of Geneva, at the heart of the valley, grew more gracefully. Within the city limits, the National Register of Historic Places lists more than 200 buildings that survive from Geneva's earliest days.

Nineteenth-century homes preside along shady streets, some still paved with cobblestones. The massive red brick 1893 courthouse towers over the business district. More than 100 shops selling antiques, artworks and other treasures tuck into old-time storefronts and renovated homes.

A Shopping Legacy

In 1835, a shop in Geneva started selling frontier supplies such as iron pots and bolts of calico. The store sat next to the spring that still gurgles along State Street, the main thoroughfare. Another business, stocking lace and fine woolens, opened about 2 years later. Shoppers have been flocking to this riverside town of 18,000 residents ever since.

Old-fashioned gaslights flank Geneva's downtown business district, which centers on State, Second and Third streets. Even the most accomplished shoppers could spend several pleasant days browsing there. You can buy fine antiques of every description and designer clothes. One shop carries only cat- and dog-themed sweatshirts, cards and other gifts for pet lovers.

Home-accessories stores showcase furnishings suitable for the Victorian and Italianate homes that line surrounding streets. But you'll also discover sleek contemporary pieces and quirky folk art. Along Third Street, pine and oak furniture that local artisans crafted fills the Wooden Nail.

Thousands of Christmas decorations pack Kris Kringle Haus, a converted historic home. Another specialty store sells only Irish imports; yet another stocks Scandinavian items exclusively.

Tasty Bill of Fare

More than 20 restaurants mingle with the shops in the business district and scatter throughout surrounding neighborhoods. Around lunchtime, a parade of shoppers moves toward The Little Traveler, a sprawling white mansion along Third Street. The mansion has been transformed into a warren of stores and dining areas. You can order shopping-lunch classics such as from-scratch chicken salad and soups.

The Mill Race Inn, another Geneva institution, overlooks the east bank of the Fox River. The heart of the rambling building is an 1842 blacksmith shop. In the 1930s, two sisters converted the old shop into a summertime tearoom. Ray Johns, a restaurateur who moved to Geneva from Chicago, bought the tearoom in 1946 and expanded it into a full-service restaurant. The eatery enjoys a fine reputation for favorites such as perfectly prepared steaks.

The inn has grown to five dining areas, including an outdoor deck that extends over the gently flowing Fox River. Ray's daughter, Rae Ellsworth, and his granddaughter now oversee the inn's operation.

Along the river's west bank, travelers settle into The Herrington Inn, built around an 1800s creamery. Original sandstone walls blend with an added third story and two wings.

Each of the inn's 40 guest rooms has its own style. In one, peach-and-blue-

The Herrington Inn is built around a creamery dating from the 19th century.

flowered upholstery and drapes complement graceful French Provincial furnishings. In another, a delicately crocheted coverlet decorates an early American four-poster.

The inn's Atwater's Restaurant, with a river view just off the lobby, is a popular spot. Here, regular diners usually start with The Herrington oysters.

Scandinavian Roots

New Englanders first settled this valley. Reports of soldiers who served here in the Black Hawk War attracted many of them. In fact, some of Geneva's oldest homes re-create styles these settlers brought with them from the East. Georgians and Greek Revivals, impeccably restored and tended, rise amid lush gardens.

By the turn of the century, Scandinavian immigrants made up half of Geneva's population, and every downtown shop employed at least one Swedish-speaking clerk. Annual festivals that attract thousands of visitors continue to celebrate that heritage.

During Swedish Days, held downtown in mid-June, you can sample traditional meatballs and sandwiches made with Swedish-baked ham at booth after booth. Other kiosks sell crafters' works.

For the festival, Graham's Chocolates, in an 1868 home along Third Street, makes floats and sundaes with lingonberries, a Swedish favorite. Visitors look on as owner Bob Untiedt and his helpers prepare a host of chocolate confections from scratch, including *skalies,* a Swedish caramel-chocolate-nut candy.

In the Congregational church's basement, artisans demonstrate rosemaling (bright, Swedish-style painting) on platters, bowls and other decorative objects. You're welcome to watch the painters while they work. Some of their creations are for sale.

The United Methodist church hosts a

Geneva teems with rewards for antiques shoppers.

RAY HILLSTROM/HILLSTROM STOCK PHOTO INC.

Swedish smorgasbord lunch. Church members prepare dishes using authentic family heirloom recipes. You can buy tickets at the door.

For the annual Christmas Walk, Santa Lucia, a traditional Swedish Christmas figure, arrives along with Santa to light the towering town Christmas tree. It sparkles on the courthouse lawn. Several of Geneva's historic homes open their doors for tours.

Neighboring Towns

If you don't see the city-limits signs, you might not realize you've left Geneva and crossed into the neighboring communities of Batavia to the south and St. Charles to the north.

A dozen or so antiques and specialty shops dot quiet Batavia, a community of 17,000.

Area antiques lovers make regular pilgrimages to St. Charles, a community of 22,000 with more than 100 antiques dealers. Most of the shops cluster in Old St. Charles, one of two downtown historic districts. The Kane County Flea Market, held one weekend a month at the fairgrounds west of town, bustles with hundreds of buyers and 1,500 dealers selling collectibles of every sort.

Century Corners, St. Charles' other historic area, climbs a hill across the river. A dozen shops occupy some of the area's mid-1800s homes.

Downtown, along a walkway that parallels the river, visitors stroll past the rocket-shaped 1940 municipal tower and a statue of a Pottawatomie chief, a tribute to the Fox River Valley's earliest settlers.

Hardly anyone can resist stopping to rub the shiny nose of one of four bronze foxes that decorate the wall of the Main Street Bridge. According to local lore, these creatures guard the valley's peaceful towns, and petting one brings you good luck.

By Barbara Morrow.

TRAVEL GUIDE

LOCATION—Northern Illinois, 35 miles west of Chicago.

LODGINGS—Standard motels in neighboring St. Charles. An alternative: The Herrington Inn, 40 guest rooms, 12 overlooking the Fox River, with fireplaces and whirlpools (doubles from $140, including a light breakfast buffet, 800/216-2466).

CAMPING—Silver Springs State Park, 1,300-acre preserve along the Fox River near Yorkville (about 30 miles southwest of Geneva), 13 sites for tent camping (630/553-6297).

DINING AND FOOD—Atwater's Restaurant at The Herrington Inn, dining with a river view (see Lodgings). The Little Traveler, a lunchtime favorite (630/232-4200). The Mill Race Inn, classic entrées in a riverside setting (630/232-2030). 302 West, award-winning fare in a former bank building downtown (630/232-9302).

SHOPPING— Kris Kringle Haus, thousands of Christmas decorations (630/208-0400). Wooden Nail, handcrafted oak and pine furniture (630/232-8696). Cats 'N' Dogs, pet-themed gifts (630/232-0001).

IN THE AREA—A trail for cycling, skating, hiking and cross-country skiing follows the Fox River for 36 miles from Aurora north to Crystal Lake. Weekend cyclists enjoy the 25-mile loop from St. Charles (just north of Geneva) south to Aurora. Mill Race Cyclery in Geneva rents bikes and in-line skates ($6 per hour, $25 per day). Information: 630/232-2833.

CELEBRATIONS—Swedish Days Festival in late June, traditional foods and music. Christmas Walk in early December, historic-homes tour, chestnuts roasting and carriage rides downtown.

INFORMATION—Geneva Chamber of Commerce, 8 S. Third St., Box 481, Geneva, IL 60134 (630/232-6060). ■

GALENA

Amid rolling riverside hills, this steamboat-era boomtown is a top Illinois visitor attraction.

Nineteenth-century brick buildings line up as stately as old-time stovepipe hats along Main Street in Galena, a town of 3,600 carved into the bluffs of northwest Illinois. The Galena River, a quiet stream today, meanders just a block east.

Among the hills that rise on all sides, grand Victorian-era homes glisten in the shimmering early-morning light. Gussied up with fresh paint and elaborate trim, these beauties stand as proudly as they did more than a century ago, when Galena boomed on lead mining and steamboat traffic from the Mississippi, 3 miles west.

This time of day, walking along the still-deserted streets, you can imagine you've stepped into the 1850s. Then, Galena was the busiest port between St. Louis and St. Paul. The DeSoto House Hotel at the center of downtown hosted guests such as Abraham Lincoln and Mark Twain. Many of the buildings haven't changed much since then. Others have been restored to look as they did before the Civil War.

Antiques and More

By mid-morning, cars vie for scarce parking spaces along Main and the surrounding streets. A steady stream of browsers strolls among the brick storefronts. More than 75 shops selling antiques, crafters' works and fanciful collectibles have replaced stores that once stocked more practical goods. Granite doorsteps, worn by decades of traffic, mark entrances, and weathered plank floors creak underfoot. Shoppers marvel at intricate tin ceilings overhead, along with old-fashioned shelves and display cases.

Shop after shop sells vintage furnishings. You'll see weathered harvest tables and pie safes that once stood in the kitchens of area farmsteads as well as intricately carved mahogany pieces like those that used to grace the homes of Galena's newly wealthy. Shoppers also will find stores brimming with smaller treasures, including

Civil War tomes and other rare volumes at Main Street Fine Books & Manuscripts.

Because of its rich history and scenic setting, Galena has become a mecca for artists. More than 20 galleries showcase regional and national artists' works. At the Carl Johnson Gallery, you'll view Johnson's watercolors of Galena scenes.

The DeSoto House Hotel still anchors downtown at the corner of Main and Commerce streets. When a group of investors built the three-story brick building in 1855, they were determined that it would be the fanciest in the Midwest. In the late 1980s, an $8 million renovation restored the hotel to its pre-Civil War grandeur. Reproductions of Victorian-era furnishings fill 55 rooms. Strolling through the lobby, you might meet General Ulysses S. Grant (Galena's most celebrated former resident, who's played by actor Paul LeGreco).

Discovering the Past

When the first European explorers made their way into the region that would become northwest Illinois, Native Americans already were mining lead from the surrounding bluffs. The glaciers that sculpted much of the Midwest never reached this region, leaving lead and other valuable minerals undisturbed on the surface or close to it.

In 1820, Congress declared the area a federal mining district, and prospectors flocked to the region around the stream known as the Fever River. A ragtag settlement of rough cabins sprouted along the riverbanks, and miners shipped lead downriver. Later, public-relations-minded leaders renamed the river and town Galena, the Latin word for lead.

By the 1830s, Galena's prospects seemed limitless. The town virtually had cornered the lead market, and Galena's boatwrights were building many of the paddle wheelers that plied the Mississippi. The population bal-

Ulysses S. Grant,
whose statue
overlooks Galena,
once was a
merchant here.

looned to more than 14,000, and residents hoped their town would be named the state capital.

Entrepreneurs and merchants built sturdy brick buildings downtown. Mining magnates and wealthy steamboat captains lavished their new riches on opulent hilltop homes, each one grander than the next.

Thanks to Galena's political influence, newly commissioned Colonel Ulysses S. Grant, a popular Mexican War veteran and Main Street merchant, was promoted to the rank of general in the Union army before he even saw action. Eight other residents, members of Grant's staff, also rose to that rank.

Frozen in Time

In the 1850s, Galena's boom began to fizzle. Railroads started transporting goods that once traveled on the Mississippi, lead production declined, and silt constricted the Galena River. Residents hoped the Civil War and increased wartime demands for lead would restore prosperity. But the turn-

around never came. By the end of the century, Galena had become a sleepy backwater. The population dwindled to around its present level.

Fewer people meant little need for new buildings, and the commercial decline left almost no money for public works—wider roads, streetcar tracks or other trappings of civic progress. But, eventually, that decades-long slump became Galena's salvation.

When preservationists and antiques lovers began rediscovering the town in the 1960s, they found a village frozen in the last century. Now, the National Register of Historic Places lists more than half of the town's buildings.

At the Galena/Jo Daviess (pronounced Davis) County History Museum in the 1858 Daniel A. Barrows mansion, exhibits trace Galena's rise and decline. Grainy photographs show the docks during the town's heyday and when the river flooded downtown. Now, a levy and floodgates that loom at the edge of the business district protect Main Street.

The Galena River, a quiet, canoeable stream, flows through town.

BOB COYLE

The Belvedere Mansion, a historic home you can tour.

DON AND PAT VALENTI/TONY STONE STOCK PHOTOS

You also can tour Galena's oldest home. The Dowling House, built of native limestone in 1826, dates to the days when Galena still was little more than a rowdy mining camp.

Grand Homes Galore

Decorated with lacy curlicues and crowned with imposing cupolas, lavish 19th-century homes decorate the hills that rise above the town's business district. You'll see graceful Queen Annes, imposing Greek Revivals, showy Gothics and architectural combinations so creative that they undoubtedly confounded Victorian-era neighbors anxious not to be outdone.

Several of the town's historic homes regularly open their doors to visitors. Steamboat magnate J. Russell Jones built the 22-room Italianate beauty that's known as the Belvedere Mansion along Park Avenue. Now open for tours, the house takes its name from its ornate "belvedere" or cupola. The home showcases opulent Victorian-era furnishings: plump, hump-backed sofas and chairs and massive ma-

hogany pieces, as well as elaborate furniture from the estate of the deceased pianist Liberace.

More than 20 historic homes now house bed and breakfasts. You can stay in a 19th-century steamboat captain's house, as fancy as a vintage paddle wheeler, or in a 20-room palace posh enough for Queen Victoria. Another 30 inns dot the countryside around Galena. Innkeepers have converted farmhouses, log cabins, country estates and even a former general store into bed and breakfasts.

Lead baron Augustus Estey spared no expense on the home that he built along High Street, now The Victorian Mansion bed and breakfast. Owners John and Mary Lou Schlenker have furnished the inn so authentically, you almost feel as if you should be wearing a Victorian costume. A graceful staircase spirals to the third floor, and antique bedsteads furnish eight rooms.

The Aldrich Guest House, a Greek Revival home along Third Street, dates to 1845. Victorian-era antiques, including a 10-foot-tall oak headboard and a claw-foot tub that was some of Galena's first indoor plumbing, decorate five guest rooms.

Future Senator Cyrus Aldrich built the Greek Revival home, but Grant's friend, future General George B. McClellan, bought it in 1850. McClellan held lavish gatherings that Lincoln, Mark Twain and Grant attended.

"The floors are original," owner Sandy Larson says. "It's a thrill to think that we're walking where those great men walked."

Beside the town's more elaborate Victorians, the house that Galena residents presented to Grant when he returned from the Civil War seems surprisingly modest. The brick two-story, now a state historic site restored to its 1868 appearance, presides along Bouthillier Street east of the river. Grant was a family man, and the house reflects his simple tastes.

The general probably heard the news that he had been elected the nation's 18th president in the somber parlor with its black horsehair sofa. Peaceful Galena, changed little since the days before the Civil War, became the Grants' escape from busy political life.

More than a century later, Galena continues to take visitors back to that gracious time.

By Barbara Morrow.

TRAVEL GUIDE

LOCATION—Illinois' northwest corner, 78 miles west of Rockford.

LODGINGS—Standard motels available. Some alternatives: Aldrich Guest House, five rooms (doubles from $90, 815/777-3323). DeSoto House Hotel, 55 rooms decorated with Victorian reproductions, all with cable television and telephones (doubles from $95, ask about packages, 800/343-6562). The Victorian Mansion, eight guest rooms (doubles from $85, 888/815-6768).

  Nearby: Chestnut Mountain Resort (8 miles southeast), 19 downhill ski runs and an array of activities (doubles from $87, 800/397-1320). Eagle Ridge Inn & Resort (8 miles east), a full-service resort sprawling across 6,800 acres with renowned golf courses, 80 lodge rooms and 340 vacation homes and condominiums (doubles from $195, ask about packages, 800/892-2269).

CAMPING—Apple River Canyon State Park (20 miles east), 300 acres of rugged terrain along the Apple River (815/745-3302). Mississippi Palisades State Park (30 miles south), 2,600 acres among the bluffs overlooking the Mississippi (815/273-2731).

DINING AND FOOD—Café Italia, hearty pastas, as well as steaks and seafood (815/777-0033). Eldorado, inventive dishes and southwest specialties (815/777-1224). Benjamin's for pizza, sandwiches and all-you-can-eat seafood on Fridays (815/777-0467).

SHOPPING—Karen's Neat Stuff, two floors of collectibles, furnishings and Christmas decorations (815/777-0911). Main Street Fine Books & Manuscripts, rare editions and more (815/777-3749). Poopsie's for pottery, decorative glass and other fine crafts (815/777-1999).

IN THE AREA—Stagecoach Trails Livery takes passengers for rides in a replica of an old-time coach like those that once traveled between Chicago and Galena. Reservations required (815/594-2423).

CELEBRATIONS—Historic Home Tour in June and September. Galena Arts Festival in July, 100 artists' works on display and for sale in Grant City Park. Galena Country Christmas on weekends, Thanksgiving–Christmas.

INFORMATION—*Galena/Jo Daviess County Convention & Visitors Bureau, 720 Park Ave., Galena, IL 61036 (800/747-9377).* ■

MORE GREAT TOWNS

Architectural treasures and crafts galore surprise visitors to the gentle small towns of Illinois.

Arthur/Arcola

These quiet villages form the heart of east-central Illinois' Amish country.

In Arcola, slightly larger of the two towns (2,700 residents) and located west of I-57, stop at the restored train depot/visitors center. You can pick up a guide to attractions, including shops along Main Street. The Flower Patch is a homey bed and breakfast surrounded by gardens.

Follow State-133 west for 9 miles to Arthur. Shops downtown stock crafts and locally made furniture. Drop in at the Dutch Oven for hearty home-style food and a wedge of from-scratch pie.

Many Amish operate cottage industries from their farms. Stop at the visitors center for a guide to businesses such as Yoder's Gazebos and the Quilt Store at Four Acres Wood Products.

Rockome Gardens, a 14-acre complex 6 miles southwest of Arcola, showcases Amish crafts. It includes gardens, a family-style restaurant, artisans' workshops and gift shops.

Location—East-central Illinois, about 25 to 35 miles south of Champaign/Urbana.

Information—Arthur Information Ctr., 106 E. Progress, Arthur, IL 61911 (800/722-6474). Arcola Information Ctr., Box 274, Arcola, IL 61910 (800/336-5456).

Elsah

Stone cottages and brick homes nestle beside bluffs along west-central Illinois' Great River Road (State-100). During steamboat days, the neighboring Mississippi was a bustling highway. But when roads and rails replaced river travel, Elsah's fortunes declined.

Today, the National Register of Historic Places lists every building along the two main streets in this town of

The Amish Country Cheese Outlet Mall, just north of Arthur in Atwood.

FRANK OBERLE

19

850. Teapots, dolls and candles share shelves at the Mercantile in the 1850s-style Green Tree Inn. Balconies of the inn's nine guest rooms, decorated in different themes, overlook the river or historic buildings.

At Elsah Landing Restaurant, diners order homemade soups, breads, pies and cheesecakes. The bakery next door specializes in cinnamon rolls.

Location—Southwest Illinois along the Mississippi, 11 miles north of Alton.

Information—Greater Alton/Twin Rivers Convention & Visitors Bureau, 200 Piasa St., Alton, IL 62002 (800/258-6645).

Geneseo

Imposing 19th-century homes and a bustling shopping district attract visitors to this northwest Illinois town of almost 6,000 residents. Settlers from Genesee County in New York state claimed this green valley in 1836.

At City Park in the center of town, a tin-roofed gazebo and band shell recall simpler times. Victorian-era homes with gingerbread trim line broad boulevards around the park. A block north, stroll beneath awnings of storefronts that house gift, specialty and antiques shops. Try the barbecued shrimp and grilled steaks at The Cellar Restaurant.

Location—Northwest Illinois, 20 miles east of the Quad Cities.

Information—Geneseo Chamber of Commerce, 100 W. Main St., Geneseo, IL 61254 (309/944-2686).

Lebanon

The Prairie State's first college was founded here in 1828. With about 3,700 residents, Lebanon remains a sleepy college town devoted to its past. More than a dozen specialty shops occupy the ornate 19th-century storefronts along St. Louis Street.

Neighboring streets pass restored homes and the McKendree College campus, shaded by towering oaks. Visit Old Main, built in 1851, and Bothwell Chapel, which dates to 1858.

Location—Southwest Illinois, about 30 miles east of St. Louis.

Information—Lebanon Chamber of Commerce, Box 204, Lebanon, IL 62254 (618/537-8420).

Maeystown

A weathered stone bridge leads into tiny Maeystown (population: 116) in a southwest Illinois valley where three streams meet. German settlers built the village to last. Now, the National Register of Historic Places lists the entire town. Steep lanes climb past a handful of shops and simple frame houses.

The refurbished 1859 mill houses a visitors center. Pick up a map that locates 40 historic buildings, including founder Jacob Maeys' 1852 homestead. The 1883 Corner George Inn, now a bed and breakfast, welcomes guests. Antiques, crafts and gifts pack the Maeystown General Store and Raccoon Hollow Handicrafts. The one-time cobbler shop now houses a Taste of Illinois, with wines from regional vineyards. Stop for ice cream at the Sweet Shoppe.

Location—Southwest Illinois, about 30 miles southeast of St. Louis.

Contact—Maeystown Visitors Information, c/o Corner George Inn, Main and Mill sts., Maeystown, IL 62256 (800/458-6020).

Petersburg

In 1836, Abraham Lincoln, a resident of the central Illinois village of New Salem, helped survey the neighboring town of Petersburg. By 1850, New Salem had all but disappeared. Petersburg along the Sangamon River prospered as the Menard County seat.

Many of the original buildings survive in this town of about 2,400 residents. The courthouse dominates a busy square, and Victorian-era homes line the steep streets. Quality crafts and antiques fill Petersburg Peddlers, also a tearoom. At the Chamber of Commerce, pick up a map of more than 50 historic sites, including the home of *Spoon River Anthology* poet Edgar Lee Masters.

The re-created village of New Salem (2 miles south) appears much as it did in Lincoln's day. Near the park, try Baby Bull's restaurant.

Location—Central Illinois, 20 miles northwest of Springfield.

Information—Petersburg Chamber of Commerce, Box 452, Petersburg, IL 62675 (217/632-7363). ∎

INDIANA

CHESTERTON • CORYDON • GREENCASTLE MADISON • METAMORA NASHVILLE • NEW HARMONY SHIPSHEWANA

In the years preceding the Civil War, Indiana became known as the "Crossroads of America." Today, more highways intersect in this state than anywhere else in the nation. Along many of those highways and byways, you can explore small towns that claim unique personalities, but share the state's special welcoming brand of Hoosier hospitality.

For information about additional Indiana small towns you can visit, contact: *Indiana Tourism Div., 1 N. Capitol, Suite 700, Indianapolis, IN 46204-2288 (800/449-4612).*

NASHVILLE

Artists and crafters, inspired by the scenery, have made this south-central Indiana town their home.

In the early 1800s, a few hardy pioneers found their way from the hills of Kentucky and Tennessee to the woodsy ridges and deep valleys of south-central Indiana. While Indianapolis mushroomed just 60 miles north, progress came slowly to Nashville and surrounding Brown County at the heart of this rugged hill country.

Settlers made what they needed, from brooms to hand-hooked rugs and homespun clothes. They also took for granted the beauty of the sweeping vistas that unfolded from almost every hilltop.

At the turn of the century, when a group of artists discovered Brown County's scenic landscape, locals wondered at all the fuss. But those newcomers changed Nashville forever. As more artists arrived and painted area scenes, visitors followed to see for themselves the countryside captured on so many canvases.

Nashville's population still hovers around 800, including more than 100 artists and crafters who now live and work here. Downtown, two galleries showcase regional artists' works, and more than 300 shops and restaurants occupy old-fashioned storefronts and 19th-century homes.

Crafts and Home Cooking

Hills rise on all sides of downtown Nashville, which rests in a hollow. Before 9 a.m., the mist that crept in overnight still shrouds the crossroads at the center of the business district. Everything is quiet, except for the clatter of plates and coffee cups on the wide front porch of the Artists Colony Inn. The wood frame hotel, painted the color of rich cream, rises above the intersection.

The inn's owner, Ellen Carter, oversees preparation of hearty breakfasts such as from-scratch biscuits topped with thick, steaming sausage gravy, and cream-cheese-filled pancakes with fresh red raspberries.

Ellen, who's the daughter of a Brown County artist, and her husband, Jay, commissioned a local artisan to craft Shaker-style furnishings for the inn's 20 rooms. A Brown County weaver fashioned the rugs that warm the plank floors. Local artists' works decorate the walls.

"We wanted to create a place with the spirit of Brown County's heritage," Ellen says.

By mid-morning, visitors stroll from shop to shop along shady walks. The Brown County Weavery, with its nubby, handmade shawls and ponchos in a rainbow of colors, occupies a century-old log cabin in a peaceful grove.

In some shops, visitors watch as the artisans work. Andy Huddleston deftly spins his potter's wheel in a white cottage that is set back from the sidewalk. The tiny building once was the summer kitchen for one of Nashville's oldest homes. Andy's plates, bowls and candleholders overflow onto benches out front.

Sunlight splashes through the windows of the Brown County Craft Gallery on East Main Street where local artisans show and sell their works. Quilts share shelves with handmade jewelry, tightly woven baskets and dozens of other creations.

Aromas from nearby restaurants remind you of old-fashioned Sunday dinners. At the Nashville House, fried biscuits and baked apple butter accompany every meal.

With its gingham tablecloths, stone hearth and log walls, the restaurant's dining room feels as cozy as an old-time farmhouse kitchen. You can order homey favorites such as fried chicken or ham steak with red gravy. Regulars save room for another specialty: gooey pecan pie.

Artists in Residence

The Brown County Art Gallery, a new stone structure, crowns a hill away from the busiest shopping area. Brown County artists show their works here

PERRY STRUSE

You'll discover more than 100 crafters and artists in Nashville and the hill country around the town.

and in the Brown County Art Guild, a converted historic home downtown.

At least a couple of days a week, a handful of members sets up easels in the gallery and paint. The artists range from veterans who've painted here for decades to talented newcomers. The painters consult with each other and happily answer onlookers' questions about works in progress or finished canvases. Paintings on the walls range from softly brushed landscapes to richly detailed wildlife renderings and angular abstracts.

The painters don't mind the interruptions. "We have a true community of artists here. That's what it's all about," one old-timer explains.

Outsiders Come to Town

Some say Brown County's art community was born near the turn of the century, when an artist named Adolph Schultz read a report about the area's beauty and decided to visit. He and a group of painter friends arrived by train and stayed in Nashville.

Residents laughed at the artists with their goatees and citified ways. To the outsiders, Brown Countians, who were content to live at an unhurried pace, seemed just as eccentric.

An Indianapolis newspaperman, Kin Hubbard, invented a cartoon character called Abe Martin, who embodied what came to be known as the "Brown County way." Coast to coast, readers chuckled at Abe's homey wisdom and country twang. But Brown County natives didn't get the joke.

Since then, residents have made peace with the character. The cartoon no longer appears in newspapers, but you'll see Abe's scruffy likeness all over Brown County. Abe Martin Lodge, just outside town at Brown County State Park, bears his name.

About the same time that painters were arriving in Nashville, T.C. Steele, perhaps Brown County's best-known artist, was building a house at the crest of a hill 9 miles west. You can tour Steele's home (House of the Singing Winds), his studio and surrounding

Visitors browse downtown Nashville.

MICHAEL VAUGHN

grounds and gardens, preserved as a state historic site. Along trails that wind through the woods and wildflower patches, visitors sample the peace that the artist found here.

Backroads Wandering

Around Nashville, bumpy routes barely two lanes wide wiggle along old creek beds and climb almost straight up to ridge tops. These twisting routes take you to tiny hamlets that have kept their backwoods names such as Bear Wallow, Stonehead and Gnaw Bone.

One road travels to Christiansburg (population: 2), little more than a crossroads with a gleaming white country church. Another byway leads to Pikes Peak, actually one of the county's flatter spots. Legend has it that the name comes from a fellow who was bound for Colorado, but ended up in Brown County instead.

On the way to Story (population: 7), the lane dips past a meadow bobbing with oxeye daisies. The Story Inn occupies the former general store, a homely, tin-sided building.

Heading north from Nashville, a little-traveled route leaves the highway and meanders to Bean Blossom Bridge, an 1880 covered span that's the state's oldest.

East of town along State-46, a double-barreled covered bridge (the only one of its type in Indiana) marks the entrance to Brown County State Park, the state's oldest and largest preserve. A 90-mile network of horseback-riding and hiking trails winds across the hills.

A smooth blacktop carries visitors through the park to some of the county's most sweeping vistas. From Hesitation Point, hills roll into the distance for 30 miles, and bluish mist, delicate as a veil, floats in the valleys. It's easy to see why artists have struggled for generations to capture scenes like this one on canvas.

By Barbara Morrow.

TRAVEL GUIDE

LOCATION—South-central Indiana, 40 miles south of Indianapolis.

LODGINGS—Abe Martin Lodge, rooms and cabins in Brown County State Park (doubles from $69, 812/988-4418). Artists Colony Inn, 20-room downtown inn opened 5 years ago and furnished with local crafters' works (doubles from $147, 812/988-0600). Cornerstone Inn, 4-year-old accommodations downtown (doubles from $95, 812/988-0300). Hotel Nashville, newer all-suite hotel a block from downtown (doubles from $124, 800/848-6274).

CAMPING—Brown County State Park, modern, primitive and equestrian sites, huge outdoor pool (812/988-6406).

DINING AND FOOD—The Nashville House, homey favorites in a cozy setting (812/988-4554). Hobnob Corner, casual cafe in an 1800s dry-goods store (812/988-4114). Old Country Store, traditional treats such as baked apple butter and sassafras tea in a shop adjacent to The Nashville House (812/988-4554).

SHOPPING—Alberts' Antique Mall, fine antiques and a bed and breakfast (812/988-2397). Brown County Craft Gallery, 50 artisans' works downtown (812/988-7058). Ruth's Garden, gardening gear, gifts and collectibles downtown (812/988-0665).

CELEBRATIONS—Annual Log Cabin Tour in late May or early June. An Old-Fashioned Holiday Family Celebration in December.

IN THE AREA—Monroe Lake, about 15 miles southwest, is Indiana's largest reservoir and the site of nationally acclaimed fishing tournaments. The lake features three public beaches, more than 400 campsites and a marina (812/837-9546).

INFORMATION—*Brown County Convention & Visitors Bureau, Box 840, Nashville, IN 47448 (800/753-3255).* ■

MADISON

Architectural treasures abound in this proud steamboating town beside the Ohio River.

The Ohio River laps a lazy refrain against the now-quiet riverfront that rims the southeast Indiana town of Madison. It's hard to imagine those early river days when this graceful community of 14,000, sheltered by towering bluffs, bustled as the gateway to the frontier.

In the 1830s and '40s, the busy port rivaled Indianapolis, and residents dreamed that their town would be the state capital. But the frontier moved west, and most of Madison's commercial dreams went with it. By then, however, some of the Midwest's finest early-19th-century homes lined the streets, and elaborate commercial buildings with arched windows and intricate cornices stood shoulder to shoulder along Main Street.

More than a century later, Madison appears much as it did during its steamboat days. But the town's attitude matches the Ohio River's lazy pace.

Madison in Bloom

The historic district claims 133 blocks. A collection of 19th-century homes, as imposing as Greek temples, reigns along flower-lined streets.

Shops that invite browsing have replaced river traders and dealers in frontier necessities, who once ruled downtown. You'll find most stores, restaurants, historic buildings and museums along Main Street and scattered in quiet neighborhoods within easy walking distance.

Along shady boulevards, early Federal-style buildings rise amid stately Greek Revivals. Striking Italianates, dressed up in lavish cornices, preside over some streets, and modest shotgun-style cottages form neat rows along others. (Some of the narrow shotgun-style structures served as hospital wards for Civil War soldiers.)

Lacy ironwork decorates homes and businesses. Many of the balconies, gates and trims of every sort were forged in early Madison's foundries. Gardens bloom on practically every available patch of earth, even in the narrow alleyways that separate buildings. Lilacs, peonies and satiny white blossoms of giant southern magnolias perfume the air in spring. By the early summer, old-fashioned hollyhocks grow tall stalks, adorned with jewel-toned, crepe-papery blossoms.

Antiques Haven

Nineteenth-century buildings house more than 30 shops. You'll discover stores packed with antiques and gifts in gracious mansions, century-old storefronts and 1800s factories.

A 140-year-old mill with walls four bricks thick houses an antiques mall. Browsers marvel at the original framework of rough-hewn oak center beams 47 feet long and more than a foot in diameter. Phil and Judy George restored a red brick cast-iron-front grocery and transformed it into The Attic, which sells gourmet foods, decorative prints, greeting cards and pottery.

You'll find landscape paintings, wildlife prints, hand-carved duck decoys and other artworks in the Clifty Creek Gallery.

Evan Sommerfeld, owner of the Old Town Emporium, stocks a selection of 18th- and 19th-century furniture and accessories, along with fine English china and delftware.

Sample classic vintages as well as special batches such as dandelion wine at Lanthier Winery, which occupies a small, refurbished 19th-century fort. You also can taste wines and tour the Thomas Family Winery in a refurbished 1855 carriage house and stable.

Historic homes and other buildings given new life as bed and breakfasts dot the center of town and cling to surrounding hillsides. Guests have the Stookey Carriage House all to themselves. The cozy structure sits in the heart of Madison's historic district. Inside, a pencil-post bed, primitive pine antiques and woven rugs mix comfortably with a rough red brick wall and wooden stable door.

TONY WALSH

Green bluffs
backdrop the
Ohio River Valley
above Madison.

The Main Street Bed and Breakfast echoes the refined air of Madison's classic Revival-style houses. The 1843 inn once was home to the Bachman family, whose son, Alois, was a Civil War hero. Now, English country antiques fill the four guest rooms.

Steamboat Days

Madison prospered almost from the day it was founded in 1809. Protected by wooded bluffs, the settlement claimed a high, dry shelf on a gentle northern bend along one of the Ohio River's most navigable stretches. The new village also perched strategically on the eastern edge of vast lands opened for settlement to the west.

At the Jefferson County Historical Society Museum, some old photos show paddle wheelers along the riverbank, trumpeting their comings and goings with raucous blasts of steam. Others picture factories that turned out goods to send downriver or over-land with westward-bound settlers.

A model re-creates the busy wharf, where workers loaded made-in-Madison goods: red and black ware from local potteries, starch, chairs and textiles from other factories. The premier industry was pork packing. "Until 1850, Madison was the biggest city in the state," curator Joe Carr says.

Town planners laid out extra-wide streets, fitting for the most important city in the state. Flush with new wealth and good fortune, riverboat captains and merchants built imposing homes and rows of stately townhouses.

But by 1860, river traffic slowed, new gateways to the west prospered, and Madison's boom economy subsided. For almost a century, the town slumbered, untouched by progress.

A Reawakening

In the 1960s, when citizens banded together in a preservation effort, they discovered a treasure trove of architec-

Take a relaxing break at the Coffee Mill Cafe.

TONY WALSH

ture. Two walking-tour maps, available at the visitors center along East Main Street, guide you to 49 restored homes and offices. Several are open for tours, including the Sullivan House, Madison's first mansion, and Dr. William Hutchings' 19th-century office building, filled with original furnishings.

The J.F.D. Lanier State Historic Site and the Shrewsbury House stand out as two of the finest homes. Both have been restored and dazzle visitors. You'll appreciate their outstanding design, craftsmanship and furnishings.

In Madison's heyday, James F.D. Lanier, a financier and railroad tycoon, and Captain Charles Lewis Shrewsbury, a river trader and meat packer, built fortunes and an intense rivalry.

Each hoped to own the most impressive riverfront mansion. They even used the same renowned architect.

The Lanier mansion's imposing columned facade and porticoed balcony command a wide view of restored gardens and the Riverfront Parkway. The Shrewsbury House is more subdued in design, but it features the most impressive spiral staircase. Steps rise from the center of the front hall and seem to float upward without visible support.

Beyond the historic district, streets climb the bluffs to views of downtown and the river valley. Even after a quarter of century living here, shop owner Judy George says, "I almost have to pinch myself to believe it's real."

By Peggy Ammerman.

TRAVEL GUIDE

LOCATION—Indiana's southeast corner, 86 miles southeast of Indianapolis.

LODGINGS—Standard motels available. Some alternatives: Main Street Bed and Breakfast, three guest rooms (doubles from $89, 800/362-6246). Schussler House, three guest rooms (doubles $90, 800/392-1931). Stookey Carriage House Bed & Breakfast, private guest cottage (double $90, open May 1– November 1, 812/265-6892).

CAMPING—Clifty Falls State Park (*see In the Area*, 812/265-1331). Falls of the Ohio State Park (55 miles west), an interpretive center and 400-million-year-old fossil beds covering 220 acres (812/280-9970). Versailles State Park (30 miles north), a 230-acre lake and surrounding park; 27-mile Hoosier Hills Bicycle Route nearby (812/689-6424).

DINING AND FOOD—The Cinnamon Tearoom, country cuisine, including roast pork seared with cinnamon apples and brandy (812/273-2367). Key West Shrimp House for seafood, frogs' legs and Key lime pie (812/265-2831). Turchino Pécora for inventive pizza and other Italian specialties (812/273-4888). The

Upper Crust Restaurant, cuisine with continental flair (812/265-6727).

SHOPPING—The Attic for prints, gourmet foods and pottery (812/265-5781). Cozy Station, a collection of toys, candles, pottery and other unusual home accessories (812/265-5757). Lumber Mill Antique Mall, vintage furnishings and collectibles in a historic mill (812/273-3040).

IN THE AREA—Hiking trails lead to waterfalls and overlooks in Clifty Falls State Park (a mile west). Stay at the Clifty Inn State Park Lodge (doubles from $69, 812/265-4135).

CELEBRATIONS—Madison in Bloom garden tour the last weekend in April and first weekend in May. Madison Chautauqua, open-air juried art festival, the fourth weekend in September. Nights Before Christmas Candlelight Tour of Homes the last weekend in November and first weekend in December.

INFORMATION—*Madison Area Convention & Visitors Bureau, 301 E. Main St., Madison, IN 47250 (800/559-2956).* ■

SHIPSHEWANA

A never-ending fascination with the Amish draws visitors to this serene country town.

In Shipshewana, at the heart of northern Indiana's Amish Country, traffic moves only as fast as the horses and buggies that share the streets with cars. One buggy, pulled by a smartly stepping bay, carries a week's worth of groceries lined up in brown bags on the seat. The driver, an Amish homemaker wearing a prim bonnet and a mid-calf-length gray dress, handles the reins as easily as drivers steer their family sedans.

A farmer, dressed in dark homemade trousers, suspenders and the broad-brimmed straw hat that most Amish men wear in warmer months, drives an enclosed wagon. A pair of squealing pigs that are probably bound for the Shipshewana auction peer through the wooden slats.

The Amish come to this village of 524 (about 25 miles east of Elkhart) to take care of business. Their buggies line up at the grocery and hardware stores and in the bank parking lot. On one corner, a group of Amish men discuss corn prices and the chances for rain, almost oblivious to the curious stares of onlookers.

Visitors flock to Shipshewana for a glimpse of Amish life. Shops sell Amish crafts, from furniture to quilts, and restaurants serve the hearty, old-fashioned specialties that the Amish favor. The weekly flea market on the grounds of the cavernous auction house south of town attracts thousands of buyers and sellers.

Amish Auctions And Home Cooking

Shipshewana started as a farming center, catering to the "Plain People," as the Amish call themselves. They make their homes in surrounding Lagrange and neighboring Elkhart counties.

The Amish, one of the largest enclaves in the U.S., traveled here to sell produce, livestock and handmade items at the weekly auction. The sale's high-quality goods—from fresh eggs and homemade bread to colorful quilts—soon began attracting outsiders.

Today, the auction takes place in a huge, white barn and on surrounding grounds along State-5 at the south side of town. The event attracts many more visitors than locals. More than 35,000 come on Tuesdays and Wednesdays to browse the 1,000-stall flea market, spread across 40 acres. You can buy everything from antiques to fresh vegetables and souvenir T-shirts.

Downtown, in the shadow of a towering grain elevator, more than 50 shops and eateries occupy spruced-up storefronts, converted homes and new buildings. Most are within just a few blocks of one another. Along broad sidewalks, flower beds and wooden barrels overflow with blooms, as if to welcome visitors.

Amid the gift and craft shops, a number of businesses serve the everyday needs of the Amish. Troyer Carriage Company manufactures horse-drawn vehicles, from the boxy buggies (the Amish equivalent of a station wagon) to jaunty two-seaters. Yoder's Hardware sells kerosene lamps, butter churns and other necessities for a life without electricity and power tools.

Hungry visitors line up in front of the Blue Gate Restaurant to sample Amish-style specialties such as fried chicken, roast beef and even fried mush. For dessert, order a wedge of old-fashioned shoo-fly pie (made with molasses), an Amish favorite.

The Amish don't necessarily eat these foods every day, a waitress explains. Cooks prepare rich, traditional dishes for their "gatherings," celebrations held for events such as weddings or barn raisings.

You can stay in homey rooms at the Old Davis Hotel, a two-story white frame hostelry that has presided over Main Street since 1891. Passersby can't resist the rockers that beckon from the shady side porch.

The hotel's first floor houses Lolly's Fabrics and Quilt Shop. Bright bolts of material in a kaleidoscope of colors

Strolling is sure to mean shopping along the streets in Shipshewana.

and patterns line shelves in one section of the shop. Another room holds quilts of every description, many made by local Amish women. You'll see traditional Amish patchworks of boldly colored geometric shapes, as well as classic designs such as the wedding ring and log cabin.

From a Buggy Seat

In the next block, handcrafted weather vanes and painstakingly hammered pots glint in front of the Old World Coppersmith. Visitors are welcome to watch the crafters at work in a studio beside the shop.

The Craft Barn, a renovated factory, holds shops crowded with more quilts, collectibles and Amish handiwork such as *lumba bubba* (rag dolls made without faces to discourage vanity). Next door, sturdy handcrafted chairs, tables and other items fill the Craft Barn Furniture Shops.

Mel Riegsecker, the owner of the barn and several other businesses, creates miniature horses and carriages that are accurate to the smallest detail.

Mel, whose father was an Amish harness-maker, started fashioning the miniatures as a hobby. Now, you can watch as Mel and a team of artisans in a workshop in the Craft Barn make handsome steeds and toy-size wagons and carriages.

Mel also operates nearby buggy rides. Visitors can tool around town in a black buggy like those the Amish drive, or ride in a white carriage complete with tufted red velvet seats fancy enough for Cinderella.

There's almost always a wait for the black buggy. "We thought people would like the white carriage best," Mel says, "but there's such a curiosity about the Amish."

A Simple Life

Driving the country roads around Shipshewana gives you perhaps the best glimpse of Amish life. On farms that divide the flat landscape into a neat patchwork, the Amish live much as their sect's founders did almost 3 centuries ago. Church rules forbid cars, electricity and other modern con-

Alvin and Else Miller operate Lolly's Fabrics in the restored Old Davis Hotel.

Amish and Mennonite volunteers built the main building at the Menno-Hof Visitors Center near Shipshewana in just 6 days.

veniences. (Codes are less strict for other branches of the faith such as many of the Mennonite sects.)

On Sundays, you'll see groups traveling by buggy or on foot to religious services held in homes. Congregations usually limit their numbers to around 20 families, and members depend on each other. If an Amish family needs a barn, neighbors gather to help build it. If church members fall on hard times, others make sure they're taken care of.

Boxy white farm homes amid the surrounding farm fields often house several generations of the same family. Amish farmers work the fields with their horse-drawn equipment. Windmills spin overhead, and homemade clothes billow on the lines beside big gardens. The rows of drying dresses on the lines can tell the female make-up of a family: Young girls wear cheery pastels, middle-age women dress in medium shades, and grandmothers wear darker colors.

Families produce much of what they need and pass old-time skills such as cabinetry and quilting from generation to generation. The more conservative Amish avoid unnecessary contact with outsiders, but they gladly sell their crafts and baked goods to visitors.

Travelers can learn more about the Amish at Menno-Hof Visitors Center south of the business district along State-5. The center, which resembles an Amish farm with a house, barn and pond, delves into Amish history.

State-of-the-art exhibits illustrate the origins of Amish and Mennonite faiths. You can walk into re-created dungeons like those in Europe, where early converts suffered for their beliefs.

The Rev. Oliver Yutzy, who helps manage the center, hopes visitors leave understanding, "The way the Amish live is an expression of deep faith."

By Barbara Morrow.

TRAVEL GUIDE

LOCATION—Northern Indiana, about 25 miles east of Elkhart.

LODGINGS—Standard motels available around Elkhart. Some alternatives: Old Davis Hotel, basic rooms in a century-old downtown establishment (doubles from $55, 219/768-7300). Country Inn & Suites, new Victorian-style motel on the north side of town (doubles from $85, 219/768-7780). Essenhaus Country Inn, a newer motel and adjacent restaurant (8 miles west of Shipshewana along US-20), decorated with country furnishings and quilts (doubles from $87, 219/825-9447).

CAMPING—Pokagon State Park (about 30 miles northeast, 219/833-2012).

DINING AND FOOD—Blue Gate Restaurant, a cafe renowned for home-style cooking (219/768-4725). Meeting House, dinner theater performances (219/768-4725). Das Dutchman Essenhaus, bustling restaurant serving Amish-style meals beside the Essenhaus Country Inn (see Lodgings, 219/825-9471).

SHOPPING—Lolly's Fabrics and Quilt Shop for quilts, sewing supplies and quilting workshops (219/768-4703). Old World Coppersmith, handmade copper and brassware (219/768-4293). The Craft Barn, toys, dolls and handcrafted furniture (219/768-4725).

CELEBRATIONS—Annual May Fest early in May. Country Christmas Open House in November.

IN THE AREA—Amish Acres near Nappanee (about 35 miles southwest) is a restored Amish farm with craft shops and a dinner theater in a renovated round barn (800/800-4942). Locally made furnishings decorate the adjacent Inn at Amish Acres (doubles from $94, 219/773-2011).

INFORMATION—The Craft Barn (a clearinghouse for Shipshewana information), Box 220, Shipshewana, IN 46565 (219/768-4725). ■

MORE GREAT TOWNS

Though the settings vary, each of these towns reminds you of when life was simpler and serene.

Chesterton

This onetime northern Indiana farming center with 9,100 residents has become an antiquers' mecca and a base for exploring nearby Indiana Dunes State Park and Indiana Dunes National Lakeshore. Downtown, made up of turn-of-the-century buildings, angles around a park adorned with a white gazebo. Two dozen antiques and specialty shops occupy storefronts and converted homes along surrounding streets. Browse Vernier Gifts for a selection of music boxes, paintings and collectibles. Yesterday's Treasures antiques mall houses 120.

Stop at Mary's Ice Cream Parlor in a Victorian house. Many visitors stay at the Gray Goose Inn, an eight-guestroom bed and breakfast on 100 acres near downtown.

Location—50 miles southeast of *Chicago City in northwest Indiana.*

Information—Porter County Convention, Recreation & Visitors Center, 800 Indian Boundary Rd., Chesterton, IN 46304 (800/283-TOUR).

Corydon

Set in southern Indiana's hills, Corydon (population: 2,700) served as the first capital. Today, the town boasts some of the state's earliest history.

The original capitol, an imposing building of locally quarried blue limestone, towers above parklike grounds. The surrounding historic district includes the home and office of Indiana's second governor and the 1800 Branham Tavern. It was built by Corydon founder William Henry Harrison, who became our ninth president. A sandstone monument preserves part of "Constitution Elm." Beneath it, leaders

Autumn color blazes amid folk-art shops in Metamora.

gathered to work on the state constitution when it was too hot to stay in the courthouse.

Shops selling gifts and antiques line Main Street. You can watch artisans at Zimmerman Glass create treasures that are shipped around the world. You'll discover the Kintner House Inn, an 1873 bed and breakfast with 15 guest rooms, within an easy walk of the business district.

The Battle of Corydon Memorial Park south of town preserves the site of the only Civil War battle ever fought on Indiana soil.

Location—Southern Indiana, 20 miles west of Louisville, Kentucky.

Information—Harrison County Chamber of Commerce, 310 N. Elm St., Corydon, IN 47112 (888/738-2137).

Greencastle

Hurrying seems out of place among turn-of-the-century storefronts along the courthouse square in this serene western Indiana college town. This community of 10,000 grew up around 160-year-old DePauw University. On the tree-studded campus, just south of the business district, bells peal from the clock tower atop an 1870s building, one of 11 historic structures on campus.

Around the square, specialty shops mingle with offices and other stores. Stop in the Almost Home Tea Room for lunch or Hathaway's for steak.

Rockers line the front porch of The Walden Inn, a newer cream-colored brick hotel at the edge of the campus, where you can dine in a Colonial setting at the Different Drummer Restaurant. Two-lane roads meander from Greencastle to 42 covered bridges, an 1880 flour mill and Indiana's highest waterfall.

Location—Western Indiana, 39 miles west of Indianapolis.

Information—Putnam County Convention & Visitors Bureau, 2 S. Jackson St., Greencastle, IN 46135 (800/829-4639).

Metamora

This tiny village (population: 97) borders the 14-mile-long Whitewater Canal, a key 1800s water highway. Metamora's pre-Civil War buildings house more than 100 shops where you can browse antiques, folk arts and crafts (some shops close on weekdays).

The sound of grinding stones echoes from the old water-powered gristmill, where the miller—face covered with fine grain dust—explains how the stones crush corn and wheat into meal.

You can stay at The Publick House and Thorpe House bed and breakfasts. Try the family-style catfish at the Hearthstone. Duck Creek Palace serves great beans and corn bread.

Visitors stroll the towpath beside the canal or ride in a horse-drawn canal boat. On May–October weekends, Whitewater Valley Railroad makes 32-mile steam-powered runs between Metamora and Connersville.

Location—Southern Indiana, 60 miles southeast of Indianapolis.

Information—Metamora Welcome Line, Box 117, Metamora, IN 47030 (317/647-2109).

New Harmony

The gentle spirit of the visionaries who founded New Harmony lingers along the streets of this town of about 850, now a mecca for artists and crafters.

In 1814, German Lutherans, who hoped to build a utopia, founded the town. Some of the clean-lined brick and frame structures date to that time. Starting at the Atheneum Visitors Center, a daring architectural creation, you can take a walking tour of 15 homes and public buildings, some furnished as they were in the early days.

Across town, the Labyrinth, a maze of sculpted bushes, symbolizes life's complexities. Shops in the business district sell antiques, vintage books and crafts.

The 90-room brick New Harmony Inn, furnished in spare Shaker style, anchors the historic district. You can dine at the adjacent Red Geranium Restaurant (try the lemon pie), Bayou Grill or Yellow Tavern (for burgers).

Location—Southwest Indiana, 35 miles northwest of Evansville.

Information—Historic New Harmony, Box 579, New Harmony, IN 47631 (812/682-4488). ■

IOWA

DECORAH • KEOSAUQUA
McGREGOR
MOUNT VERNON • PELLA

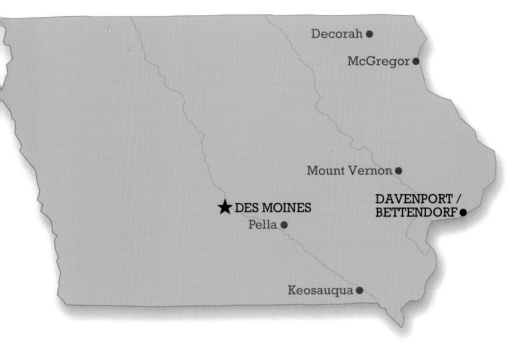

Decorah

McGregor

Mount Vernon

★DES MOINES

DAVENPORT /
BETTENDORF

Pella

Keosauqua

Stick the tip of a pin in an Iowa road map, and you'll probably obscure at least two or three of the many small towns that sprinkle the Hawkeye State. Though some say Iowa's wealth comes from its rich, black soil, the small towns and the people who live in them rank among this state's treasures.

Whether backdropped by the rolling hills of Grant Wood country, scenic river bluffs or gentle rural countryside, these proud communities savor life at a pleasurable pace. You can learn about their immigrant heritage at local museums, join in annual festivals, eavesdrop on friendly gossip at the corner cafe or simply stroll the sidewalks and acknowledge the welcoming smiles and hellos that make you glad you came.

For information about additional Iowa small towns you can visit, contact: *Div. of Tourism, Iowa Dept. of Economic Development, 200 E. Grand Ave., Des Moines, IA 50309 (800/345-IOWA).*

DECORAH

Known for its Nordic heritage, Decorah celebrates its roots among the hills of northeast Iowa.

The knobby limestone palisades and forested hills of northeast Iowa's Upper Iowa River Valley reminded early Norwegian immigrants of their homeland. So many Norwegians settled here, in fact, that Decorah became known as Iowa's "Little Norway." The community served as a stopping-off point for thousands of Norwegian settlers headed for homesteads to the north and west.

Today, this tidy college town of 8,700 continues to celebrate its heritage. A nationally acclaimed museum preserves Norwegian heirlooms and hosts authentic festivals. Shops brim with Nordic crafts and Scandinavian imports. At local restaurants, you can try authentic old-country dishes.

Wooden cutouts of *nisses* (Norwegian elves) peek from windows around town, and bright-red Scandinavian-style mailboxes decorate porches. Newcomers quickly learn to say *"Velkommen!"* (welcome) and to exclaim *"Uffda!"* (an all-purpose expression of surprise or dismay).

A Proud History

Named for a Winnebago chief, Decorah thrives as the seat of Winneshiek County, a top dairy-farming county. The river forms a half-circle around the town's business district. Wooded bluffs rise on one side of downtown, and gentle hills dotted with homes curve upward on the other.

Along Water Street, the main thoroughfare, coffeehouses, a co-op grocery store, and gift and antiques shops tuck into vintage buildings. During summer, you can sample the region's bounty at the Farmer's Market, held near City Hall on Wednesday afternoons and Saturday mornings.

The Vesterheim Norwegian-American Museum complex, which includes a one-time luxury hotel and other historic buildings, spans most of a downtown block (*Vesterheim* means "Western Home"). The museum, the oldest and largest of its kind in the

U.S., opened its doors in 1877 and has helped make Decorah a national center for recording and preserving Norwegian traditions. In addition to the carefully restored historic buildings, you'll see collections of pioneer furnishings, colorful costumes and rosemaling (decorative Scandinavian painting).

The museum started with a small collection at Luther College. The school moved here from Wisconsin in 1861, helping establish Decorah as a Norwegian stronghold. Once the training center for thousands of Lutheran clergy, the college now is a private liberal-arts school. Set on a hilltop, the campus still offers a major in Scandinavian studies, along with one of the area's best views.

In 1933, the museum moved downtown. Its collection now includes more than 20,000 artifacts and heirlooms. Displays trace the immigrants' journey from the rough ocean crossing to the hardships of early settlement.

In the soaring ship gallery, immigrant art depicting maritime themes serves as the backdrop for the *Tradewind*. Two Norwegian brothers crossed the Atlantic in the crude 25-foot sailboat in 1933.

Behind the main museum building, an outdoor section includes a house and a three-story mill from Norway, the 1852 home of a Norwegian pastor and an 1880 log school.

Next door, the light and airy Dayton House Norwegian Cafe serves authentic Norwegian dishes such as *lapskaus* (a beef-and-pork stew) and sells imported foods such as flatbreads and jams. Merchandise you can buy in the adjacent shop ranges from books that poke good-natured fun at Norwegians to specialized tools for woodcarving.

Strolling Through Yesterday

Stop in at the chamber of commerce office along Winnebago Street for a brochure that takes you on a walking tour of the Broadway-Phelps Park His-

PERRY STRUSE

Nestled among the hills, Decorah reminded early settlers of Norway.

toric District. Broadway Street, which runs along the ridge south of downtown, travels up a gradual incline to Phelps Park. There, a limestone walkway leads to an overlook with a commanding view of Decorah and the surrounding valley.

The town's founders built Decorah's first churches, public school and homes—from cottages to mansions—on the hills above town to escape floods, which periodically inundated the river valley. Today, the district almost is a museum of Midwest architectural styles. You'll discover regal Queen Annes, Dutch Colonials, English cottages and Prairie-School styles standing side by side along the shady streets.

Visitors can tour the Porter House Museum, a native brick Tuscan-Italianate home that's listed in the National Register of Historic Places. A rock wall, made from tons of stones and semiprecious gems such as agates, amethysts and crystals, surrounds the house. The home's one-time owner, Adelbert Field Porter, who was an artist and naturalist, built the wall. Inside the house, you can view Porter's extensive collections of stamps and mounted insects.

Outdoor Exploring

The rugged beauty of the river valley and the countryside around it attracts outdoors enthusiasts during every season. In town, Dunning's Spring Park surrounds the site of one of Decorah's early mills. The waterfall and trail make the park a popular spot for picnicking, hiking and picture-taking.

In the warmer months, inner tubes and canoes float the Upper Iowa River, gliding past wooded bluffs and palisades. Canoeists and tubers rank the stretch between Decorah and Kendallville (20 miles northwest) as one of the state's most scenic. Area outfitters rent canoes and inner tubes.

Just south of town, the State Fish Hatchery welcomes visitors. You can picnic beside the pool where Siewers

Dancers in costumes attract crowds at Nordic Fest.

COURTESY OF THE VESTERHEIM NORWEGIAN-AMERICAN MUSEUM

Spring pours down from a bluff or watch the fish feed in the hatchery's large trout-rearing tanks.

The local chamber of commerce publishes a brochure of city trails and county bike routes. Prairie Farmer Bike Trail covers 18 miles from Calmar (10 miles south of Decorah) to Ridgeway (8 miles west).

Celebrating Nordic Customs

Vesterheim is the focal point of this community's rollicking annual three-day Nordic Fest, held the last full weekend in July. Residents, the college and the museum cooperate to produce one of the world's most authentic Norwegian festivals outside Norway.

Residents dressed as trolls—important figures in Norwegian folklore— roam downtown. Dancers and singers in ornate traditional costumes perform, and dozens of artisans demonstrate their Norwegian crafts. You can watch knife-makers, woodcarvers, weavers and china-painters at work.

At food booths downtown, visitors sample Norwegian fare. Here's your chance to try *lefse* (mashed potato bread) or *søtsuppe* (a sweet soup). *Lutefisk* is only for the intrepid (it's codfish soaked in lye).

The event attracts thousands with Norwegian heritage and others who just want to join in the fun. Many festivalgoers take part every year, filling area lodgings and prompting some residents to open their homes to guests. Most who experience Decorah's velkommen want to return again.

By Rebecca Christian.

TRAVEL GUIDE

LOCATION—Iowa's northeast corner, about 62 miles southwest of La Crosse, Wisconsin.

LODGINGS—Standard motels available. Some alternatives: Montgomery Mansion Bed and Breakfast Inn, four guest rooms (doubles from $45, 800/892-4955).

CAMPING—Decorah Municipal Campground just off US-52 along Pulpit Rock Road. Information: 319/382-9941.

DINING AND FOOD—Dayton House Norwegian Cafe for Old World dishes (319/382-9683). Mabe's Pizza, a favorite with Luther College students (319/382-4297). The Clarksville Diner, an authentic 1930s establishment that resembles a railroad car, for hearty fare such as meatloaf and locally raised capon with dressing (319/382-4330).

SHOPPING—Vanberia International Gifts, with an overflowing inventory of crystal, Hummel figurines, music boxes, dolls, Christmas items, craft and sewing kits, cookware and all manner of things Scandinavian

(319/382-4892). Vesterheim Museum Sales for troll figurines, books about Norwegian heritage and imports from Norway (319/382-9682).

IN THE AREA—The Bily Brothers Clock Exhibit now occupies the home where Czech composer Antonin Dvorak stayed when he visited the tiny town of Spillville (about 10 miles south). The bachelor brothers spent years carving a collection of elaborate timepieces, some more than 7 feet tall. The charming town also features the Old World Inn restaurant, known for Czech specialties, plus a church and museum. Town information: 319/562-3569.

CELEBRATIONS—Nordic Fest the last full weekend in July. Norwegian Christmas at the Vesterheim Norwegian-American Museum. Handel's *Messiah* at Luther College the first weekend in December.

INFORMATION—*Decorah Area Chamber of Commerce, 111 Winnebago St., Decorah, IA 52101 (319/382-3990). Eastern Iowa Tourism Assoc. 216 W. 4th, Vinton, IA 52349 (800/891-3482).* ■

PELLA

Long-standing traditions color everything Dutch in this inviting central Iowa community.

In the mid-1880s, the promise of religious freedom spurred Pastor Hendrik Scholte to lead 800 Dutch immigrants to central Iowa. After paying $1.25 an acre for 18,000 acres of what they were told was fertile prairie, only woods, tall grass and a half-built abandoned cabin greeted them.

The newcomers named their spartan settlement Pella ("City of Refuge") and hastily built straw-roofed sod huts in preparation for their first Iowa winter. Five generations later, that village has grown into a thriving community of 9,712 that serves as the business hub for the surrounding farm country. But Pella's residents also remain true to their Netherlands heritage.

Dutch facades decorate the shops around the square, where you can buy lace and blue-and-white delft china from the old country, as well as Dutch pastries and old-country sausage.

Along surrounding streets, sidewalks and doorsteps almost gleam, as if they just were freshly scrubbed. Curtains of Dutch lace, as delicate as snowflakes and in patterns almost as varied, peek from windows. For the Tulip Time festival each May, all of Pella celebrates its Dutch ancestry, and thousands of visitors become Dutch for a day or two.

A Windmill Welcome

A miniature windmill stocked with visitor information occupies one corner of the manicured town square, known as Central Park. The Tulip Tower, 65-foot twin pillars that memorialize Pella's Dutch founders, rises above one side of the square.

At regular intervals, the chimes of the Klokkenspel, a half block east of the of the square in a courtyard along Franklin Street, ring throughout the business district. At regular intervals, visitors gather to watch the street scrubbers, wooden-shoe maker and other 4-foot-tall carved figures taken from Pella's history cavort in the window below the clock tower. Tiles in the courtyard also depict scenes from Dutch history.

Modeled after old-time architectural styles popular in Holland, facades on surrounding buildings in red brick and a cheerful assortment of colors reach improbable peaks. Some stairstep neatly to square crowns, while others swirl upward in curves.

You'll discover most shops that cater to visitors along Main Street on the east side of the square, along Franklin on the square's south side, and onward a block to the east. Some shops stock antiques and gifts you might not find anywhere else. Other establishments sport tongue-twisting Dutch names, and their wares give clues to the life Pella's ancestors left behind.

If you would like a pair of authentic wooden shoes, you can stop in at one of four stores, including the Ben Franklin just east of the square. Nearby, DePelikaan stocks still more authentic clogs, along with delft and other china and stoneware in traditional blue and white. Dutch lace decorates the walls. You can order swaths of "spring tulip," "trellis loop" or any of 20 other patterns.

Two more stores also sell this imported fancywork. Lace curtains are a Dutch tradition, one shopkeeper explains. Homemakers prized cleanliness and, supposedly, delicate lace window coverings allowed passersby glimpses of homes' tidy interiors.

Dutch Treats

At In't Veld's Butcher Shop along Main Street facing the square, shoppers line up to buy rings of Pella bologna. Don't ask butcher Stan Bogaard how it's made; he keeps the recipe a closely guarded secret.

Mid-morning and again at around 3 p.m., many residents still observe koffieklets, traditional times for coffee and visiting. It's standing room only at the butcher shop's tables and at downtown restaurants.

Return to Pella as it used to be at the historic village.

Across the square at Jaarsma Bakery, Ralph Jaarsma arranges neat rows of crisp almond cookies, apple tarts and S-shaped filled pastries known as Dutch letters. Even when Ralph's grandfather worked here in the early 1900s, the bakery was a local legend.

Sharing Pella's Past

A walking-tour map guides visitors to other legacies of Pella's earliest days. Stroll past a brick home that is one of the town's oldest, the McClatchy House, a restored Gothic masterpiece, and a log cabin that survives from the community's early days.

The mansion that founder Hendrik Scholte built still dominates the north side of the square. To ease the heartbreak of leaving their homeland, the pastor promised his wife, Mareah, he would build her a grand house in the New World like the one they'd left behind. Within a year, the 23-room white frame house rose in the center of Pella.

Now, the grand house is open for tours. Inside, you'll see antique furnishings and the Scholte family artifacts. A stout iron chest with an intricate locking system once held the Dutch colonists' precious guilders. In spring and summer, thousands of tulips and other flowers bloom amid majestic old trees in the garden that the Scholtes planted behind the house.

Visitors also can tour the turn-of-the-century Pella Opera House. The restored theater hosts shows by nationally known performers.

East of the square, 21 buildings scatter across the parklike grounds at the historic village. Red brick walkways lead to century-old structures. Some of them numbered among Pella's first, and others were moved to the site.

The complex includes homes, a blacksmith shop, mill and bakery. You can see the shards of Mareah Scholte's delftware embedded in one of the village's walkways. Unfortunately, the china was broken during the family's

The Tulip Time festival celebrates Pella's Dutch past.

JOAN LIFFRING-ZUG BOURRET

Stop for meats and conversation at In't Veld's Butcher Shop.

PERRY STRUSE

rough ocean crossing.

In the village, visitors can peer into a sod hut like those that Pella's earliest residents built for themselves. You'll marvel that the settlers made it through those early winters. An 1851 log cabin appears more comfortable, with its massive stone fireplace and simple, sturdy furnishings.

The Van Spanckerens Store contains an 1899 switchboard. Nearby, the library showcases a collection of Iowa law books and Dutch clothing. Displays explain that an outfit's decorations and colors revealed the origin and standing of its wearer.

At the Werk Platts, you'll see machinery used to make wooden shoes; the sturdy *klompen* line up in the factory window. The village also preserves the home of Wyatt Earp. The legendary lawman spent much of his boyhood in Pella.

On the south side of town, the Rolscreen Museum showcases the early products the Pella Corporation made. Founded here in 1925, the company now is one of the nation's largest window manufacturers.

Bos Landen, an 18-hole championship golf course designed by Dick Phelps, spreads across 350 acres of rolling terrain. The course name means "land of woods" in Dutch, and towering oak and hickory trees cast long shadows on its green fairways.

Tulip Time

Resolutely, residents decided to hold the first Tulip Time celebration during the depths of the Depression. The decision came too late to plant real tulips, so carved wooden flowers decorated Pella for that first festival in 1935.

The next year, volunteers planted bulbs all over town. The tulips bloomed on schedule, launching one of the largest Dutch festivals celebrated in the U.S.

More than 60 years later, the whole town blooms by mid-May. Thousands of tulips brighten the historic village, sway along walkways and decorate yards. Residents don colorful costumes—some to take part in the annual parade, and others just to watch.

The fun begins with the honorary *burgemeester's* stern proclamation: "The streets are dirty!" Brigades of broom-wielding scrubbers scamper onto the pavement, brushing and sweeping furiously until the streets pass a mock inspection.

Klompen dancers wearing colorful Dutch costumes and wooden shoes then sashay down the main streets. Four hundred local youngsters spend weeks practicing intricate steps to authentic dances.

After they pass by, floats, including one carrying the festival queen and her court, parade around the square to cheers of the crowd. From booths and carts, vendors sell sausages, cookies, pastries and Dutch pancakes called *poffertjes*, sticky with butter and sugar.

The Pella Historical Village also comes alive for the event with crafts-people demonstrating old-time skills. You can watch wooden-shoe-makers and a blacksmith at work.

Local church congregations welcome visitors with huge dinners. The diners line up for heaping portions of Dutch favorites such as "spiced" beef (roasted meat flavored with allspice) or Iowa standards such as ham and scalloped potatoes. One church holds a special Sunday service at which costumed choir members sing in Dutch.

Almost as soon as visitors depart and the tulip blooms wither, an army of volunteers already is planning and preparing for next year's Tulip Time celebration. Visitors enjoy a day or two of watching folk dancers and sampling the authentic foods. But for many Pella residents, Dutch traditions remain a way of life.

By Debbie Leckron Miller.

TRAVEL GUIDE

LOCATION—Central Iowa, 40 miles southeast of Des Moines.

LODGINGS—Standard motels available. Holiday Inn Express, new motel across from Bos Landen golf course (doubles from $69, 515/628-4853). The Clover Leaf bed and breakfast, with four guest rooms in a restored home (doubles from $50, 515/628-9045).

CAMPING—Lake Red Rock (*see In the Area*), 400 campsites, most with hookups (515/828-7522).

DINING AND FOOD—Central Park Cafe, Pella bologna on a kaiser roll, traditional Dutch "spiced" beef and from-scratch lemon meringue and other pies (515/628-4042). DeSnoepwinkel, chocolate shop and tearoom with salads, sandwiches, soups and tasty desserts for lunch (515/628-1222). In't Veld's Butcher Shop for Pella bologna, homemade bratwurst and beef franks (515/628-3440). Jaarsma Bakery, Dutch letters, apple bread and other treats (515/628-2940). Vander Ploeg Bakery, Dutch letters and other pastries (mail orders, 515/628-2293).

SHOPPING—DePelikaan for delftware, lace and other Dutch imports (515/628-9479). Red Ribbon Antique Mall, 30 dealers with merchandise ranging from primitives and vintage china to furniture (515/628-2181). Van Den Berg's for dolls, plates, figurines and other popular collectibles (515/628-2533).

IN THE AREA—Lake Red Rock (4 miles west) is Iowa's largest Corps of Engineers reservoir and a favorite with pleasure boaters and anglers. The 14-mile Volksweg Bike Trail, a paved pathway, circles the lake, traveling through woods and across wooden bridge. Borrow a bike at neighboring Bos Landen Golf Club (800/916-7888). Recreation areas along the lake offer camping, dam tours and campfire programs (515/828-7522).

INFORMATION—*Pella Convention & Visitors Bureau, 518 Franklin St., Pella, IA 50219 (888/GO-DUTCH).* ■

MORE GREAT TOWNS

This trio of towns shines like gems amid Iowa's rich, rural landscapes.

Keosauqua

With 1,000 residents, Keosauqua is the largest of a cluster of historic riverside villages that bloomed in southeast Iowa during steamboating days.

The pride of Keosauqua, the Hotel Manning, rises a stone's throw from the riverfront. The three-story red brick building with white trim was constructed in stages, beginning in 1839.

Visitors can tour the Federal-style courthouse, the seat of business for surrounding Van Buren County since 1843. It's the oldest continuously operating courthouse in the state.

A handful of antiques and specialty shops occupy some of the storefronts along three-block-long Main Street. Browse Top of the Hill Antiques and stop for home-style cooking at Corner Cafe or River Bend Steak and Pizza.

A few miles southeast of town, plan to explore the riverside towns of Bentonsport, Bonaparte and Farmington.

Location—Southeast Iowa, about 55 miles west of Burlington.

Information—The Villages of Van Buren County, Box 9, Keosauqua, IA 52565 (800/868-7822).

McGregor

Framed by forested Mississippi River bluffs, McGregor grew up in a corner of northeast Iowa around a ferry landing. By the mid-1800s, the downtown bustled with saloons, merchants and shipping concerns. Now, galleries and shops selling antiques and crafts abound along Main Street. River Junction Trading Company specializes in gear and clothes from the Old West.

The Ringling brothers of circus fame spent some of their boyhood here, perfecting backyard big-top stunts. The local museum includes displays about the Ringling family and Andrew Clemens, a local artist who created elaborate pictures using grains of sand.

Pleasure boaters ply this stretch of the Mississippi River. Vacationers can rent houseboats and pontoons here and in nearby river towns.

At dinnertime, head for the White Springs Supper Club south of town, a

Connie Davenport welcomes you to her Hotel Manning in Keosauqua.

RUSS MUNN

local institution along US-18, renowned for barbecued ribs and catfish.

Several of the vintage buildings in McGregor have been preserved as bed and breakfasts. Little Switzerland Inn occupies a century-old structure that once was the headquarters of the local newspaper. The River's Edge, an early 1900s white frame home, overlooks the Mississippi.

Pikes Peak State Park southeast of town perches on a bluff above the river. Zebulon Pike found this overlook before he made his more famous discovery in Colorado.

Location—Northeast Iowa, about 60 miles north of Dubuque.

Information—McGregor/Marquette Chamber of Commerce, Box 105, McGregor, IA 52157 (800/896-0910).

Mount Vernon

The spires of Cornell College's King Chapel peek through the trees as you approach Mount Vernon, surrounded by eastern Iowa farm country. Fields and pastures give way to this hilly town of 3,500 residents, with a shady New England look.

In the mid-1800s, Mount Vernon and the college sprang up along a military road between Dubuque and Iowa City. Well-kept Victorian homes and red brick campus buildings trimmed in white now are listed in the National Register of Historic Places.

The refurbished brick storefronts that cluster along First Street house numerous specialty and antiques shops. You can stop in at The Perfect Blend, where owner Ann Booth sells freshly baked Scottish shortbread. You'll also find a variety of gift items there, from locally carved walnut nativity sets to hand-knitted scarves. Billibob's, serving lunch and dinner, is known for steaks and sandwiches.

At the chamber of commerce office along First Street, you can pick up a free brochure that directs you along the avenues branching off from this main artery. Three bed and breakfasts in Mount Vernon welcome travelers: Engelbrecht's, Cottage Garden and Inn Among the Trees.

Location—Eastern Iowa, 15 miles east of Cedar Rapids.

Information—Mount Vernon Chamber of Commerce, Box 281, Mount Vernon, IA 52314 (319/895-8214). ∎

Jim Boeke seems to live in the 1880s at River Junction Trading Company in McGregor.

PERRY STRUSE

KANSAS

ABILENE • COUNCIL GROVE
DODGE CITY
FORT SCOTT • GARNETT • LINDSBORG

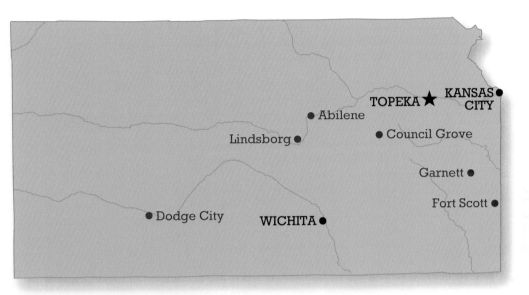

Traditions of hospitality characterize small towns located across the Sunflower State. Many of these communities have been hosting travelers for more than a century. Some began welcoming visitors 150 years ago as important stopping-off points along the Santa Fe Trail and other historic frontier "highways" to the West.

Intriguing tales of rowdy cowpokes and dusty longhorns, six-shooters and lawmen, and tenacious sodbusters sprinkle the pasts of these communities. Re-creating and chronicling those early days continue to be a highlight when you visit many of these small Kansas towns today.

For information about additional Kansas small towns you can visit, contact: *Kansas Dept. of Commerce & Housing, Travel & Tourism Div., 700 S.W. Harrison St., Suite 1300, Topeka, KS 66603-3712 (800/2-KANSAS).*

ABILENE

Cattle drives brought life to this Kansas town, now known as Dwight D. Eisenhower's home.

A land speculator laid out Abilene on the central Kansas prairie in the early 1860s. The town's name, taken from the Bible, means "city of the plains."

For several years, Abilene didn't amount to much. Then, in 1867, the Kansas legislature opened the state to cattle drives. Thanks to some political maneuvering, tiny Abilene on the banks of Mud Creek became Kansas' first cow town.

Over the next 5 years, cattle drives brought 3 million longhorns across the Chisholm Trail from Texas to Abilene, where they were shipped east by rail. In their wake came droves of rowdy cowboys, merchants and shippers eager to make their fortunes in the prairie's latest boomtown.

Taverns and bawdy houses sprang up along the muddy streets. Lawman James Butler "Wild Bill" Hickok kept a raucous sort of order, but Abilene still gained a reputation as the wickedest town in the West. The cattle shipping ended in 1872, after only 5 years, partly because residents wanted to eliminate all the trouble the drives brought to town.

Today, you'll see little evidence of the wild cowboy past in this town of 6,400. But grand Victorian-era homes, gracious reminders of cattle fortunes made here, still parade along broad, shady streets. President Dwight D. Eisenhower grew up in one of the community's simpler frame homes. The town's Eisenhower Center traces our 34th president's modest beginnings, as well as his public life.

Old-Time Downtown

Heading south to Abilene's compact downtown, Buckeye Avenue takes you past block after block of sprawling historic homes.

In the business district, which clusters around the intersection of Buckeye and Third Street, handsome 19th-century brick buildings stand shoulder to shoulder. You can browse and buy at three antiques malls housed in ren-

ovated storefronts, including one with 100 dealers. Everything from vintage saddles to pioneer furniture and valuable glassware is for sale.

Local artists' and crafters' creations stock several stores. The Heritage Shoppe displays regional paintings and fine crafts. Area potters' pieces star at the Farmers and Drovers Gallery.

Vanilla-scented candles perfume the air at Genny's Country Cupboard. The shop is in an 1890s shoe store. An old-time tin ceiling soars above a collection of afghans, crocks painted with cheery Kansas sunflowers and other home accessories. From the deli at the rear of the store, order a plate-size, from-scratch cinnamon roll or a local Czech favorite, *bieroch* (ground beef, spices and shredded cabbage that's baked in a golden crust).

Be sure to stop at the 1928 Union Pacific Depot, a restored Spanish Colonial-style landmark along Second Street. It's been transformed into a visitors center. In summer, 1-hour guided van tours depart from out front.

Guide Lynda Alstrom points out sites such as infamous Texas Street. "More than 30 saloons, gambling houses, et cetera—and you can guess what et cetera means," she says with a wink—"crowded that street. Not a single building remains."

"Little Town Of Mansions"

More than 100 grand, historic homes stand along tree-lined streets, earning Abilene the nickname "Little Town of Mansions." Along Buckeye, you can't miss the traffic-stopping Seelye Mansion, a whitewashed 1905 Georgian gem that spans an entire block.

A patent-medicine magnate built the 25-room home, which boasts 11 bedrooms, a bowling alley and a ballroom. Tiffany of New York designed the tiled hearth in the mansion's Grand Hall and one of Thomas Edison's original light fixtures hangs above the mantel. Guides lead visitors on daily tours.

Kansas' five-star general, former president and hometown hero proudly overlooks the Eisenhower Center.

Most of the town's restored homes preside along Buckeye and Third Street. But if you venture onto side streets such as Vine or Spruce, you'll discover other treasures.

An Abilene banker built the opulent 23-room Lebold-Vahsholtz Mansion along Vine Street. An Italianate brick beauty dating to 1880, the home is the town's oldest. The Vahsholtz family conducts tours by appointment. Inside, you'll see all the trappings of Victorian wealth, from lavish furnishings and draperies to a set of pearl-handled sterling silver flatware.

Tucked away side by side along Spruce Street are two historic homes, which both have been renovated as bed and breakfasts. Spruce House and Dora Theay Ah's welcome visitors with old-world graciousness.

Abilene's other bed and breakfast, Victorian Reflections along Third Street, joins the lineup of restored showplaces. A selection of the finest open their doors to visitors for the annual Christmas Tour of Homes.

You can dine in a Victorian setting at one of Abilene's finest renovations, the Kirby House along Third Street. Irish immigrant Thomas Kirby, who built a bank that still stands downtown, erected the Italianate masterpiece in 1885. After it had been converted to apartments a century later, Terry Tietjens and his now-deceased twin brother, Jerry, restored the mansion and opened it as a restaurant.

Inside, Victorian touches remain: a parquet entry floor, leaded-glass windows and a maple fireplace mantel in the parlor. Guests dine on every level, including in the tower, where there's a cozy table for two. New owners Ed and Betsy Varner often lead diners on tours of the sprawling house.

A Tribute to "Ike"

On the south side of town, the Dickinson County Historical Museum

Visitors can tour Abeline's Lebold-Vahsholtz Mansion.

showcases Abilene memorabilia, including Wild Bill Hickok's badge and gun. For $1, you can take a nostalgic ride on the hand-carved C.W. Parker Carousel. Built in Abilene at the turn of the century, the old-fashioned carousel still operates daily.

Next door, the Museum of Independent Telephony tells the story of the small telephone companies that sprang up across the country when Alexander Graham Bell's original 17-year patent expired. In Abilene, Cleyson L. Brown started the United Telephone Company, which now is the local division of Sprint Corporation.

One of the museum's displays traces the telephone's evolution, starting with the early hand-cranked models. Another exhibit displays the first pay telephones. One phone even has a slot for silver dollars.

Across the street sprawls the Eisenhower Center, a fitting tribute to Abilene's most notable hometown hero: five-star general and later President Dwight D. Eisenhower. A film in the visitors center recounts "Ike's" life story and explains the workings of the library. Thousands of private contributions paid for the massive limestone structure.

A simple white frame foursquare stands on the grounds. Ike and his parents, along with his five brothers, lived there from when Ike was 2 years old until he left for West Point in 1911. The president's father, David, worked as a mechanic in a local creamery, and his mother, Ida, sold vegetables from her garden to help support the family. Eisenhower, his wife, Mamie, and one of their sons rest in a limestone chapel on the center grounds.

Speaking to a hometown audience, the president once declared, "The proudest thing that I claim is that I am from Abilene." You'll understand what he meant when you walk the streets of this peaceful prairie town.

By Debbie Leckron Miller.

TRAVEL GUIDE

LOCATION—Central Kansas, 90 miles west of Topeka.

LODGINGS—Standard motels available. Neighboring century-old homes transformed into bed and breakfasts: Dora Theay Ah's, with one guest room (double from $55, 785/263-0266), and Spruce House Bed and Breakfast, a century-old stucco home with three guest rooms (doubles from $60, 785/263-3900). Victorian Reflections, four guest rooms in a historic mansion (doubles from $55, 785/263-7774).

CAMPING—Covered Wagon RV Park, sites with full hookups, near the Eisenhower Center (800/864-4053).

DINING AND FOOD—Genny's Country Cupboard, sandwiches and homemade cinnamon rolls in a deli at the rear of the shop downtown (913/263-4714). Kirby House, nine dining rooms in a Victorian-era mansion, serving classics such as steaks and seafood (785/263-7336).

SHOPPING—Bow Studio and Gallery, tiles handmade from local clay (785/263-7166). Downtown Antique Mall, more than 100 dealers (785/263-2782). Farmers and Drovers Gallery, pottery and other regional artworks (785/263-0240).

IN THE AREA—The Abilene and Smoky Valley Railroad makes excursions into the surrounding farm country. Passengers ride in a century-old restored wooden diner or an open-air car (785/263-1077).

CELEBRATIONS—Chisholm Trail Days in October. Christmas in the Depot, Friday before Thanksgiving. Christmas Tour of historic homes and craft show in December.

INFORMATION—*Abilene Convention & Visitors Bureau, 201 N.W. Second St., Abilene, KS 67410 (800/569-5915).* ■

LINDSBORG

Scandinavian traditions, *Dala* horses, *ostkaka* and a warm *valkommen* greet visitors here.

More than half of the residents of this central Kansas town (population: 3,200) trace their ancestry to Swedish immigrants. But strolling Lindsborg's quiet streets, you might guess that the whole town claims Scandinavian roots. Bright red-orange *Dala* folk-craft horses, a Swedish symbol, decorate almost every doorstep and storefront. Signs everywhere proclaim *valkommen* (welcome).

Bakeries sell old-country favorites such as Swedish tearings and *ostkaka* (a Scandinavian cheesecake). Restaurants serve Swedish pancakes, saucy meatballs and from-scratch rye bread. For festivals, residents don bright Scandinavian costumes and twirl to tunes from their ancestors' time.

The Swedes who settled here more than a century ago brought a love of the arts, fine crafts and music. Those traditions still thrive at Bethany College, founded by Lindsborg's earliest settlers. The parklike campus on the north side of town is home to the renowned Birger Sandzen Gallery, and the college stages nationally acclaimed musical performances.

You'll find artists at work in area studios and galleries that display their creations. Hand-crafted treasures, from traditional Swedish painted pieces to furniture and ceramics, fill many of the downtown shops.

Dalas and Other Discoveries

Freshly painted cornices almost shine on the carefully tended vintage brick buildings downtown. The eight-block area centers on the intersection of Main and Lincoln streets.

Glinting under the cloudless Kansas sky on a sunny afternoon, the spire of Bethany Lutheran Church rises above the wide, brick-paved streets, which are laid out in a neat grid pattern. A hardware store, pharmacy and clothing shops mingle with more than a dozen craft and specialty shops.

You'll see Dala horses of every description: miniatures for Christmas tree ornaments, Dalas you can hang on your front door and three-dimensional Dala horses big enough for a child to ride. According to Swedish legend, 19th-century carvers in the furniture-making province of Dalarna started crafting toy horses from wood scraps. Lindsborg has adopted the cheery horse as its official symbol.

At Hemsløjd imports shop, you can watch artisans carving and painting the horses. Then, order one to take home. The shop creates Dala-horse-shaped signs, usually in red, emblazoned with Scandinavian surnames. But artisans also regularly paint signs with names such as Alvarez and Murphy.

"In Lindsborg," says crafter Ken Sjogren, "you don't have to be Swedish by birth. You can be Swedish by choice."

More Local Delights

Nearby, Swedish Crafts stocks more traditional artisans' works, including intricate wheat weavings, carved wooden figures and brightly painted platters and bowls.

Anderson Butik is another must stop. You can buy almost everything Swedish there, from lingonberries to Scandinavian china and maps. At Prairiewood Gallery, furniture-makers construct clean-lined Swedish-inspired tables, chairs and other furnishings from native pine.

The Courtyard Gallery displays the creations of more than 40 regional artists. You'll see everything from watercolors and prints to pictures that local artists fashioned from the feathers of ring-neck pheasants.

At the Swedish Crown, diners sample hearty old-country farm fare. "Ours is very much Swedish country food," says owner Mark Speer. Besides Swedish meatballs and other standards, the restaurant's extensive menu also lists dishes such as *tallrik*

ROY INMAN

Window-shopping along Lindsborg's flower-filled streets.

(meatloaf that's made with ham, pork, ground beef and spices).

The Swedish Country Inn, a 1920s hotel renovated as a bed and breakfast, is a favorite of visitors. Cheery pastels and sleek pine furnishings imported from Sweden decorate the inn's 19 guest rooms. For breakfast (open to the public), the inn serves an authentic smorgasbord, complete with herring and Swedish pastries.

Reminders of the Past

After the Civil War, Lindsborg's founders paid $2.25 an acre for a fertile tract in the Smoky Hill River Valley. Before building permanent homes, the group constructed a building that could be used as a church and a school.

In 1881, the pastor, Carl A. Swensson, founded Bethany College. Ten students attended classes. That same year, Swensson directed a group of church members determined to learn George Frideric Handel's *Messiah* in a spring performance. The production became an annual event.

More than a century later, 350 singers, some who travel hundreds of miles, make up the Bethany College Oratorio Society. Members perform the *Messiah* and Johann Sebastian Bach's *St. Matthew Passion* during a 7-day festival held the week before Easter. Other musicians also perform during the celebration, and regional artists exhibit their works at the Birger Sandzen Memorial Gallery on Bethany's campus.

Reminders of Lindsborg's early days survive at the McPherson County Old Mill Museum along the river on the south edge of town. Visitors can walk through the three-story brick Smoky Valley Roller Mill, restored to working condition. For the Millfest each May, the 1800s machinery rumbles again, and costumed interpreters demonstrate 19th-century skills such as blacksmithing on the museum grounds.

The complex's 11 other historic buildings ring a grassy park. The sunny yellow Swedish Pavilion, an imposing frame building, was moved

Dancers perform downtown at the Lucia Fest.

LARRY FLEMMING

Colorful Dala horses decorate buildings all around Lindsborg.

ROY INMAN

to Lindsborg from the 1904 St. Louis World's Fair. Inside, visitors view the interior of one of the area's oldest churches. You also can see a display of Swedish musical instruments and artifacts such as old photographs and early tools. They were handed down from the community's early settlers.

Bethany Academy, built in 1879 as the town's first school, and the railroad depot that served Lindsborg for almost a century stand nearby. The complex also preserves the area's oldest frame buildings—a courthouse and post office that were moved from southwest of town—and an 1870 log cabin that Swedish pioneers built.

Grand Celebrations

From the earliest days, Lindsborg's Swedish population quietly continued observing traditions they'd brought from the old country. In recent decades, their celebrations have started attracting visitors eager to sample the town's Swedish heritage.

The Midsummer's Day Festival in June salutes the arrival of longer, milder days with Maypole dancing and a smorgasbord of traditional foods.

Svensk Hyllningsfest, which is held every other fall, honors the founders of this central Kansas prairie town.

At that 3-day celebration, visitors line up for helpings of Swedish standards such as home-baked rye bread and *rokt lax* (smoked salmon). Crafters demonstrate their skills, including woodcarving and Dala-horse painting. Swedish cooks share their secrets to preparing classic dishes.

Lucia Fest, which is held in mid-December, ushers in the Christmas season. Carols and a special ceremony honor St. Lucia, a Christian martyr who, according to legend, appeared to save a starving Swedish village. A local girl, chosen to portray Lucia, wears a crown of candles. Carols and a ceremony mark the symbolic bringing of light to winter's darkest days.

For the town's festivals, many residents wear authentic costumes that they've carefully preserved or painstakingly duplicated. Designs indicate the home province of the person who wears the costume. Many of the traditional Swedish vests and full skirts are red—a favorite color in a land of long, cold winters.

You don't have to be Swedish to join in. Residents who have Spanish, Irish and other roots also dress up and learn the dances and songs. Local schools teach Swedish folk music, and a high school group regularly travels to Sweden. A group of Lindsborg residents meets weekly for coffee and conversation—in Swedish.

In fact, Lindsborg's citizens have so carefully preserved the customs their ancestors brought to this community long ago that, it's said, more old-time traditions live on here than in many villages in Sweden.

By Debbie Leckron Miller.

TRAVEL GUIDE

LOCATION—Central Kansas, about 70 miles northwest of Wichita.

LODGINGS—Standard motels available. An alternative: Swedish Country Inn, 19 rooms in a renovated hotel decorated with Scandinavian-style furnishings (doubles from $66, including breakfast, 785/227-2985).

CAMPING—Malm's RV Resort, 45-acre campground with hookups and two lakes (785/227-2932).

DINING AND FOOD—Main Street Grill & Bakery, for Swedish pancakes (785/227-3908). Swedish Country Inn (see *Lodgings*), breakfast smorgasbord open to the public (785/227-2985). Swedish Crown Restaurant, Swedish dishes and regional favorites (785/227-2076).

SHOPPING—Anderson Butik, for lingonberries, home accessories and other Swedish imports (785/227-2356). Hemslöjd, to buy Dala horses and watch crafters at work (800/779-3344). Prairiewood for furniture and other local artisans' works (785/227-3927). Swedish Crafts, crystal and other imports (785/227-2311).

IN THE AREA—For a sweeping view of the Smoky Hill River Valley, follow the gravel road to the top of Coronado Heights, 3 miles northwest of town. It's said to be the northernmost point that the explorer Francisco Coronado reached in his travels. A castle-shaped shelter and lookout built as a 1930s public works project tops a ridge that rises sharply over 26 acres of surrounding virgin prairie. The castle makes the perfect sunset picnic spot.

CELEBRATIONS—Millfest, tours of the historic mill and demonstrations of old-time skills, in May. Midsummer's Day Festival in June. Lucia Fest, a Swedish Christmas festival, in December. *Svensk Hyllningsfest,* founders' day celebration, every other fall.

INFORMATION—*Lindsborg Chamber of Commerce, 104 E. Lincoln, Box 191, Lindsborg, KS 67456-0191 (785/227-3706).* ∎

MORE GREAT TOWNS

The history of the Old West and frontier life still looms large in many Kansas communities.

Council Grove

Stores, hotels and other businesses sprang up more than 150 years ago in this central Kansas town, one of the main staging areas for the 800-mile-long Santa Fe Trail. Many of Council Grove's early buildings, constructed of durable honey-colored limestone, survive today. In fact, the entire town of 2,300 has been designated as a National Historic District.

A shelter east of the Main Street bridge protects the stump of Council Oak. Representatives of the Osage tribe and the U.S. government met in its shade to sign a treaty guaranteeing safe passage on the trail.

Seth Hays, a great grandson of Daniel Boone and a cousin of Kit Carson, built the Hays House Tavern along Main Street. Surrounded by trail memorabilia, diners feast on panfried chicken and prime rib. About a block north, the 1870s Cottage House Hotel has been restored as a comfortable bed and breakfast.

Visitors also can tour the old Kaw Mission, Seth Hays' home and other historic sites around town.

Location—Central Kansas, about 55 miles southwest of Topeka.

Information—Council Grove Convention & Visitors Bureau, 200 W. Main St., Council Grove, KS 66846 (316/767-5882).

Dodge City

Cowboys and millions of dusty longhorns ruled this southwest Kansas town in the 1870s and '80s. Since then, Dodge City has grown into a cattle center of 21,100 residents. But the spirit of the original frontier settlement survives at the Boot Hill Museum, a block of reconstructed buildings along Front Street.

Exhibits in shops chronicle 1870s frontier life, as well as the exploits of famous citizens such as Wyatt Earp, Bat Masterson and Doc Holliday. While you're waiting for one of the three daily "shootouts," you can ride in a stagecoach, watch a blacksmith hammer horseshoes, or sip sarsaparilla amid original furnishings at the bar of the Long Branch Saloon.

The museum, a couple of blocks west of downtown, even incorporates a

The stage line takes you back 120 years along Dodge City's Front Street.

real cemetery. A few wooden grave markers reinforce its reputation as a boots-on burial ground.

Downtown, El Capitan, a statue of a fierce-looking longhorn, surveys the intersection of Wyatt Earp Boulevard and Second Street. It's another reminder of when Dodge City was a small community on the frontier.

Location—Southwest Kansas, about 155 miles west of Wichita.

Information—Dodge City Convention & Visitors Bureau, Box 1474, Dodge City, KS 67801 (800/OLD-WEST).

Fort Scott

From a bluff, the restored Fort Scott military post watches over its namesake southeast Kansas town (population: 8,500). Before the Civil War, the fort served as a base for elite troops known as Dragoons. Later, it became one of the most important outposts on the original Kansas frontier.

After the Civil War, former officers settled in Fort Scott, opening downtown businesses and building homes befitting their new merchant status. Just beyond the fort's grounds, specialty and antiques shops now fill a number of 19th-century storefronts.

Restored "painted lady" Victorians and Italianate homes line shady brick streets. Trolley tours take you to sites around town, including the fort, where you'll see 20 buildings along the parade grounds. You can tour officers' quarters, barracks and other buildings. Dragoons drill during special events.

Location—Southeast Kansas, 73 miles south of Kansas City.

Information—Fort Scott Chamber of Commerce, Box 205, Fort Scott, KS 66701 (800/245-FORT).

Garnett

When you visit this southeast Kansas town of 3,200, you'll discover seven antiques stores, including three on the square that surrounds Garnett's 1902 red brick Romanesque courthouse.

The same Kansas architect who designed the castlelike courthouse also planned the Kirk House bed and breakfast, a Colonial Revival mansion with five guest rooms. Visitors join locals at The Pantry for home-style dining.

Plan to tour the 1880 Harris House and to see the Walker Art Collection at the public library. You also can stroll through the parks along three lakes that border town and hike a section of the Prairie Spirit Trail. An 18-mile stretch passes through town.

Location—Southeast Kansas, about 70 miles southwest of Kansas City.

Information—Garnett Chamber of Commerce, 134 E. Fifth Ave., Garnett, KS 66032 (785/448-6767). ∎

Dragoons drill on the parade ground at Fort Scott.

LARRY FLEMMING

MICHIGAN

ALLEGAN • CHESANING • FRANKENMUTH
MANISTEE • MARSHALL
PETOSKEY • ST. IGNACE • SOUTH HAVEN

• SAULT STE. MARIE

• St. Ignace

• Petoskey

• Manistee

Frankenmuth •
• Chesaning

• GRAND RAPIDS
★ LANSING
• Allegan
• South Haven
DETROIT •
Marshall

Michigan claims the distinction of being the only Midwest state bounded on three sides by the Great Lakes. In fact, the state's name, loosely translated from an Ojibwa word, means "large lake." Some of Michigan's small towns, located along or near the lakeshore, have links to those vast inland seas. Others take their character from the state's rich mix of settlers who came to better their lives by establishing farms or working in Michigan industries.

For information about additional Michigan small towns you can visit, contact: *Travel Michigan, Box 30226, Lansing, MI 48909 (888-78-GREAT).*

PETOSKEY

Sparkling shore views and exceptional shopping are just two attractions of this lakeside town.

More than a century ago, lake steamers and trains began bringing summer visitors to this inviting town of 6,000 in the northwest corner of Michigan's Lower Peninsula. Today, Petoskey, located along Little Traverse Bay, lulls visitors into a vacation mode with the ease of a practiced hostess.

The Gaslight Shopping District bustles just steps from the bay. Old-fashioned street lamps on black iron posts line the six blocks of Victorian-era storefronts. Bright awnings flutter in the steady lake breeze, and flower boxes overflow with geraniums and petunias. From time to time, shady benches tempt even the most dedicated shoppers to sit and rest awhile.

Waterfront Park hugs the bay and Petoskey Marina. White herring gulls dip and soar among banners waving from the masts of sailboats bobbing in their slips. Sunbathers claim patches of warm sand on the mile-long beach that rims the turquoise lake. Gathering here to watch the sunset has become one of the most anticipated events of the day.

Gaslight District Discoveries

More than 80 shops selling everything from artists' works to the latest in resort wear and souvenir moccasins line the six-block Gaslight District.

For a glimpse of Petoskey's past, stop at Symons General Store, the town's first brick building, constructed in 1870. You'll probably see regular customers chatting on a bench on the pillared front porch. Inside the store, baskets hang from the high tin ceilings, and old-fashioned shelves, bins and cases hold fine cheeses, meats, mushrooms and other regional delicacies. If owner Lynn Symons isn't out fishing, she'll help you pack a picnic to carry down to the shore.

Stop in at American Spoon Foods, a gourmet food company dedicated to creating specialties from Michigan fruits and vegetables. Delicacies you can sample such as Red Haven Peach Preserves line up on the shop's tasting table.

Browse galleries such as Ward & Eis. The shop, with a solarium and a view of the bay, showcases a variety of works by 200 artists. Fine Native American pieces are a specialty. Whistling Moose Studios features wildlife art and handcrafted works. At the Pottery Lodge, you can choose handcrafted crockery, then paint it yourself. Gallery prices range from less than $10 to more than $10,000.

The white wooden exterior of Andante, a restaurant on the side of a hill along Bay Street, looks refreshingly cool beneath the massive maple trees. Windows of a side dining room open to the bay.

Pennsylvania Park forms a green oasis in the heart of town. Stately hardwoods spread like canopies overhead, and flowers bloom along the walkways. Picnic tables stand in the shade. On some summer afternoons, bands play lunch-hour concerts.

Petoskey Stones And Hemingway Lore

In the 1892 Chicago and West Michigan Railroad Depot west of the marina, Little Traverse Historical Museum explores the area's past. Exhibits tell the story of the Ottawas, the area's first settlers. You'll see artifacts such as handmade birch-bark boxes decorated in intricate porcupine-quill designs. Petoskey, founded in 1852 by a Presbyterian missionary, takes its name from Ottawa chief Petosega.

Other museum exhibits focus on the early 1900s, when forests of giant white pine covered the region. Loggers built mill towns and lake ports to process and ship mountains of timber. By the mid-1870s, loggers had felled the last of the tall trees. Railroads soon began bringing carloads of wealthy vacationers, hoping to escape the heat in cities farther south.

Visitors marvel at the museum's pride: a 300-pound Petoskey stone. You'll find Michigan's state stone (it's

Petoskey's favorite shopping stretch: the Gaslight District.

350-million-year-old fossilized coral) only in waters of the bay and along Lake Michigan's northwest shore. Beachcombers sometimes discover much smaller Petoskey stones along the waterfront in Magnus Park.

The museum also honors the area's favorite son, Pulitzer Prize-winning author Ernest Hemingway, who spent most of his first 22 summers at his family's cottage along nearby Walloon Lake. Here, "Papa" married his first wife, Hadley Richardson, and gathered materials for some of his early books, including the Nick Adams stories.

Papers and mementos recall that period of the author's life. A walking tour through the city's historical district takes you past Eva Potter's rooming house, where Hemingway lived in 1919 and 1920.

A Sister Cottage Colony

On the north side of Petoskey, salmon-colored sidewalks distinguish adjoining Bay View, a community founded as a Methodist retreat in 1875. More than 400 summer cottages, lavishly adorned with gingerbread trim, Victorian turrets and pillared porches stand along winding streets shaded by majestic hardwoods.

Bay View began as a collection of tents, but soon visitors built elaborate summer homes on the natural terraces overlooking the lake. By the turn of the century, Bay View included a chapel, a hotel and a library. Notables such as Helen Keller, orator and presidential candidate William Jennings Bryan and educator Booker T. Washington addressed summer meetings here.

With waitresses in prim Victorian dress, Stafford's Bay View Inn recalls the graciousness of those summers long ago. Claim one of the wicker rockers overlooking the bay before venturing inside.

Stafford Smith, who started as a busboy at the inn years ago, often greets guests. Now, he owns this restaurant and the elegantly restored 81-room Stafford's Perry Hotel in Petoskey.

Another of Bay View's original hotels has been restored as the Terrace Inn, a three-story Queen Anne with 44

At Mitchell Street Pub & Cafe, manager Dennis Peruzzi (center) treats owners Jerry and Diane Ellman.

JOHN WILLIAMS

guest rooms and a dining room. During the months of July and August, the inn also hosts classical music concerts, recitals and lectures.

Outdoor Exploring

The deep waters of Little Traverse Bay and dozens of inland lakes, rivers, parks and preserves surround Petoskey. You'll discover more than 20 public golf courses within an easy drive. Miles of golden sand beckon swimmers, sunbathers and rock hounds.

From the Bay Marina, you can book fishing charters or rent a boat. The area's inland lakes and rivers also attract pleasure boaters, anglers and canoeists.

Campers and hikers head for Petoskey State Park, with its inviting mile-long beach, hiking trails and modern and primitive campsites. Ten Little Traverse Conservancy Nature Preserves, dotting the five-county area around Petoskey, provide more hiking, guided nature walks and other programs for outdoor enthusiasts. In early summer, naturalists also lead wildflower walks.

To appreciate all of the vacation pleasures in and around Petoskey, you're sure to be tempted to stay longer than you planned. That's just part of the lure of this gracious town that takes pride in its tradition of hospitality.

By Dixie Franklin.

TRAVEL GUIDE

LOCATION—Northwest corner of Michigan's northern Lower Peninsula, 67 miles northeast of Traverse City and 260 miles northwest of Detroit.

LODGINGS—Standard motels available, including national chains. Some alternatives: Stafford's Bay View Inn, 31 rooms in a historic 1886 inn (doubles from $118, 800/258-1886). Stafford's Perry Hotel, 81 rooms in 1899 hotel at the edge of the Gaslight District and Pennsylvania Park (doubles from $69, 800/737-1899). The Terrace Inn, restored 1910 Victorian with 44 rooms in Bay View (doubles from $76, 800/530-9898). Apple Tree Inn, 40 rooms in a newer motel, with indoor pool and whirlpools (doubles from $86, 616/348-2900).

CAMPING—Petoskey State Park (4 miles east), 305 acres along Little Traverse Bay, with sand beach and forest. Fisherman's Island State Park (19 miles southwest), 2,678 acres along Lake Michigan, with beaches to prowl for Petoskey stones. Michigan parks information: 800/44-PARKS.

DINING AND FOOD—Andante, gourmet fare overlooking the bay (616/348-3321). Mitchell Street Pub & Cafe, casual dining (616/347-1801).

American Spoon Foods, a host of delicacies made from Michigan ingredients (800/222-5886). Stafford's Bay View Inn, down-home meals and tempting desserts in Bay View (810/258-1886).

SHOPPING—Symons General Store (616/347-2612). Ward & Eis Gallery, original artworks (616/347-2750).

IN THE AREA—Across Little Traverse Bay from Petoskey, the town of Harbor Springs follows the shore. Steep bluffs border the deepest natural harbor along the Great Lakes. Wealthy vacationers have been coming to Harbor Springs for generations. The town has become an upscale artists' community, boasting galleries and chic gift shops. Information: *Petoskey/ Harbor Springs/Boyne Country Visitors Bureau (address below).*

CELEBRATIONS—National Morel Mushroom Hunting Festival in May. Little Traverse Bay Historical Festival in July. Jaycees Juried Art Show in August.

INFORMATION—*Petoskey/Harbor Springs/Boyne Country Visitors Bureau, 401 E. Mitchell, Petoskey, MI 49770 (800/845-2828).* ■

MARSHALL

Restoration and preservation make this town an architectural gem to explore.

A townwide dedication to preserving the past led to massive restorations in this serene south-central Michigan community. Today, even a patch of peeling paint or a crumbling brick is hard to find.

Marshall discovered historic preservation long before it became fashionable, and restoration has continued here for more than half a century. This community, perhaps more than any other in the Midwest, resembles a picture-book 1800s town.

Houses in almost every 19th-century style parade along the shady boulevards. You'll see block after block of stately, columned Greek Revivals, regal Italianate villas and Queen Annes, resplendent in turrets and curlicues. At the west end of Michigan Avenue, Marshall's main thoroughfare, a fountain splashes at the center of a grassy common. Along the broad boulevard, Victorian-style facades, with tall windows and cornices as fancy as lace petticoats, house gift and antiques shops that visitors can't resist.

New York Founders

Ask almost any Marshall resident how so much of the past has survived, and you're likely to get a detailed account of the town's history. It's as if knowing Marshall's story—down to exact dates—were a requirement for living here. In case anyone forgets a pertinent fact, more than 40 plaques have been posted around town, noting significant sites and important dates.

In the 1830s, a land speculator from New York state bought parcels of land where Rice Creek meets the Kalamazoo River. Then, wealthy families from upstate New York settled here and built the first gristmill. They located their new village in the center of Calhoun County. They named that new town Marshall (after Chief Justice John Marshall), and it became the county seat.

Unlike most pioneers, these New Yorkers had little interest in tilling the land. They were speculators, hoping to buy property and resell it at a profit. The settlers established quality schools and other institutions similar to the ones they'd known in communities on the East Coast.

Makeshift accommodations simply wouldn't do for travelers to this forward-thinking town. The National House Inn, with its massive hearth and cozy rooms, began welcoming guests in 1835. The inn, grand for its time, now is Michigan's oldest and operates as a bed and breakfast. Authentic 1800s color schemes—salmons, soft blues and greens—complement antiques and country-style furnishings in the 16 guest rooms.

Capital Fever

In just eight years after its founding, Marshall grew from a handful of log cabins into a town full of imposing mansions. The biggest boom came in the 1840s, when community citizens assumed their town would be designated as the state capital.

Resident and state Senator James Wright Gordon was so confident Marshall would be chosen that he built a governor's mansion. When Lansing received the designation instead, Gordon moved into the home on South Marshall Street himself. Spruced up with fresh paint, the Greek Revival house still stands today. Residents call the neighborhood that surrounds it "Capitol Hill."

The town leaders did manage to snare a lucrative Michigan Central Railroad machine shop. Marshall's future seemed assured until an 1872 fire wiped out most of the town's industrial area, and the railroad yards moved to another town. Businessmen lost everything, and the economy couldn't rebound. Though wealthy residents, some making their money in patent medicines, lived quietly in Marshall's grand homes, the town settled into a genteel decline.

Historians credit 1920s Mayor

Musicians entertain at La Pietra House during one of the home tours in Marshall.

Harold Brooks, a manufacturer of hernia trusses, with sparking the town's restoration movement. Brooks owned and renovated more than a dozen buildings and brought attention to Marshall's architectural treasures. Preservationists founded one of the nation's most active historical societies. Home tours, which now attract thousands of visitors, started in Marshall three decades ago.

Antiques and Victoriana

In the town's once-bustling business district, no one seems in a rush these days. An old-fashioned dime store sells a little bit of everything. At the local hardware store, you can get free advice about plumbing or painting.

Visitors meander among brick storefronts that showcase vintage furnishings or ribbon-and-lace-trimmed accessories that would satisfy even the fussiest Victorian matron. Fragrant candles, dainty tea sets and lacy linens fill Serendipity, an inviting shop along West Michigan.

Nineteenth-century furniture packs the Marshall House Antique Centre in what once was part of an 1838 hotel. Late-1800s china cabinets, trunks and glassware crowd every corner. Another shop, J.H. Cronin Antiques, specializes in vintage signs and assorted advertising memorabilia.

In a one-time hotel southeast of

Hans and Nancy Schuler in the Inner Circle Room at Schuler's.

RICHARD HIRNEISEN

Fountain Circle, Schuler's of Marshall, a dining institution for more than 50 years, serves dishes such as its delicious signature prime rib, freshly baked breads and irresistible desserts. Try the towering ice cream pie topped with hot caramel sauce.

Along East Michigan, a cast-iron-fronted 1868 structure houses the American Museum of Magic. By appointment, owner Elaine Lund shows off posters, tricks and antique props, which her late husband, Robert Lund, collected.

Walking Tours

The historical society makes its home in the Honolulu House, one of Marshall's most unusual buildings. A former U.S. consul to the Sandwich Islands (now Hawaii) reportedly built the house to resemble one he owned there. The result: a structure that amazed his neighbors with its Oriental-looking central tower and wide gallery. It's adorned with Victorian gingerbread that was intended to look Hawaiian.

Furnishings from the era during which the house was built still decorate the home, and tropical murals splash across the walls. A free walking-tour guide that you can pick up at the home locates more than 100 historic houses and buildings that visitors can view around town.

The tour takes you to gems such as the VanHorn-Perrett-Stagg House, a Gothic Revival built in 1860, and Oak Hill, an opulent Italianate mansion that dates to 1858.

Most of the historic buildings continue to be private homes. A selection of the finest houses open their doors for tours in September and again for the town's annual Christmas Walk in December. Homeowners love to show their hard work to hundreds of admiring visitors.

"We feel as if the town just loaned us these marvelous homes to take care of," the owner of an 1886 Queen Anne says proudly. "The homes actually belong to everyone."

By Steve Slack.

TRAVEL GUIDE

LOCATION—12 miles southeast of Battle Creek in south-central Michigan.

LODGINGS—Standard motels available. Some alternatives: National House Inn, Michigan's oldest inn, with 16 guest rooms (doubles from $87, 616/781-7374). McCarthy's Bear Creek Inn, a country estate with 14 guest rooms (doubles from $65, 616/781-8383).

DINING AND FOOD—Schuler's of Marshall, known for prime rib and rich desserts (616/781-0600). Louie's Bakery, scrumptious sweet rolls, breads, pies and other freshly baked treats (616/781-3542).

SHOPPING—J.H. Cronin Antique Center, advertising memorabilia and vintage furniture (616/789-0077). Marshall House Antique Centre, late 1800s furnishings and glassware in a historic building (616/781-7841). Serendipity, Victorian and country accessories (616/781-8144).

IN THE AREA—Cornwell's Turkeyville U.S.A., 6 miles north of Marshall, is a onetime family farm turned into a restaurant complex. The establishment serves turkey every which way, from roasted with all the trimmings to "sloppy Tom" sandwiches. Cornwell's Dinner Theater features musical productions and a buffet starring roast turkey and dressing (616/781-4293).

CELEBRATIONS—Garden Club Tours in July. Historic Homes Tour in September. Christmas Walk in December.

INFORMATION—*Marshall Area Chamber of Commerce, 109 E. Michigan Ave., Marshall, MI 49068 (800/877-5163).* ■

FRANKENMUTH

The flavor of Old World Germany lingers in this popular holiday-loving town.

A storybook atmosphere enfolds this community of 4,400 along the banks of the Cass River in central Michigan farm country. The Bavarian Inn towers over downtown like a castle from the pages of a German fairy tale. Alpine chalet-style buildings and peak-roofed cottages line the business district, and a new covered bridge spans the river. Sidewalks and doorsteps look freshly scrubbed. In season, geraniums nod in pots and window boxes.

Bronner's Christmas Wonderland, the world's largest Christmas store, dominates the south edge of town. Two downtown restaurants, the Bavarian Inn and Zehnders, serve renowned family-style chicken dinners that draw diners by the thousands.

Those attractions, along with dozens of shops selling everything from collectibles to German sausages and woodcarvings, draw more than 3 million visitors every year. That makes Frankenmuth one of Michigan's most visited communities. But, at heart, this town remains an old-fashioned German village with strong ties to old-country values and traditions.

Missionary Beginnings

In 1845, when a group of Lutheran missionaries from the Bavarian province of Franken set up camp along the Cass River, only loggers and Chippewas lived amid the dense forests that covered central Michigan. The determined band dubbed their new settlement Frankenmuth, which means "courage of the Franconians."

As lumbering cleared the land, the pioneers turned to farming. A mill that still towers along the Cass River ground locally grown grain. A brewery that produced hearty German beer also rose along the riverbank.

In those early days, worshipers attended services in a tiny log cabin. In 1880, the congregation built a massive brick church, a Gothic masterpiece with a towering white steeple. Tall stained-glass windows chronicle the struggles of the missionaries and the history of the town. More than 150 years after those missionaries arrived, St. Lorenz Church still holds a weekly service in German.

At the historical museum downtown, grainy sepia-tone photographs and excerpts from immigrants' diaries and letters tell the story of the community's difficult early years. Even after generations of prosperity, residents still treasure their heritage. The school teaches German, and many families speak it at home. You'll meet residents with a hint of an accent.

Sunday Chicken Dinners

Frankenmuth remained a quiet farming center until its location, along the state's main north-south artery, began bringing visitors to town. The Fischer Hotel offered clean rooms and tasty all-you-can-eat fried chicken dinners. Though demand for the hotel's rooms dwindled, families continued to make the long drive from Detroit and other cities on weekends just for the meals.

In the 1950s, Wally Bronner opened a Christmas decorating shop beside his sign-making business. Shoppers loved it and came in droves. They provided new customers for other long-standing businesses with roots in German traditions such as woodcarvers and sausage-makers. New shops opened in the business district, selling gifts, fudge, glassware and almost anything customers might want to buy.

The Bavarian Inn was remodeled to resemble a building from the old country. Servers dressed in colorful skirts and authentic-looking lederhosen. Local leaders agreed that new and renovated buildings would echo alpine-style architecture.

Annual celebrations such as the Bavarian Festival each June have grown into major events that attract thousands of visitors. Polka music rings through the streets, and revelers consume kegs of beer and tons of traditional bratwurst and apple strudel.

The historic Frankenmuth Flour Mill and general store.

Under the Glockenspiel

At regular intervals, the 35-bell carillon peals in the clock tower atop the Bavarian Inn. The Pied Piper and other intricately carved storybook characters pop out from behind a bronze door. The music never fails to work its magic on the town. Within minutes, streams of visitors converge on the inn's parking lot. Shoppers gladly put down bags stuffed with parcels to watch the show.

More than 100 shops line Main and surrounding streets and cluster around Bronner's at the edge of town. One Main Street store sells cuckoo clocks, beer steins and other German imports. Hand-knitted sweaters and plump, wool-filled comforters crowd another. Original paintings, dollhouse miniatures and hand-carved wooden toys fill other shops. At Schnitzelbank Woodcarving Studio, visitors are welcome to watch crafters at work.

Downtown, you can tour the Frankenmuth Brewery and sample rich German beers. At other shops, fudgemakers shape huge slabs of the gooey confection. You're invited to watch.

Visitors can walk through the kitchen of Willi's Sausage Haus, where master German sausage-maker Willi Becker oversees preparation of more than 100 varieties. Guides explain the flour-grinding process at the restored Frankenmuth Flour Mill.

Other factories, where you can watch cheese-making or even take a pretzel-twisting class, cluster on the south edge of town near Bronner's.

Crowd-Pleasing Fare

By late morning, groups start gravitating toward Zehnders and the Bavarian Inn. They're located across the street from each other at the center of downtown. Zehnders' early American decor complements the building's Greek Revival style.

When you visit the Bavarian Inn, also owned by the Zehnder family, you'll feel as if you've walked into an old-time German beer garden.

Wally and Irene Bronner at their Christmas Wonderland.

Checkered cloths drape the tables, and roving accordion players serenade you.

Even though the restaurants sometimes serve thousands of dinners daily, no one seems rushed. Chicken dinners arrive with mounds of from-scratch potatoes and the restaurants' trademark stuffing. You also can sample traditional German favorites such as Wiener schnitzel and sauerbraten. For dessert? Black Forest cake, of course.

Year-Round Yule

Displays lighted year-round lead to Bronner's Christmas Wonderland, a sprawling complex as big as four football fields. Inside, an astounding 260 trees sparkle with miles of lights and 6,000 different kinds of ornaments from all over the world. You can buy everything you need to trim a tree in traditional Scandinavian fashion or stage a Japanese-style Christmas celebration. An army of animated Santas, elves and reindeer helps bring all of Bronner's displays to life.

Wally Bronner, who's the patriarch of the family-owned operation, makes sure all the glitter doesn't overshadow the holiday's spiritual meaning. Bibles come in 30-plus languages, and you can choose from more than 500 styles of nativity sets.

Next to the huge store, the Bronners built the non-denominational Silent Night Memorial Chapel, a replica of a historic church near Salzburg, Austria, where the namesake carol first was performed. Plaques engraved with the carol and translated into 100 languages line the walk that leads to the chapel.

Wally and his wife, Irene, often greet their customers, making sure they find what they need. During the holiday season, the couple leads sing-alongs in the auditorium next door. They never considered leaving such chores completely to others. In Frankenmuth, Wally says, "We pride ourselves on welcoming visitors as if they were guests in our homes."

By Barbara Morrow.

TRAVEL GUIDE

LOCATION—Central Michigan, 86 miles northwest of Detroit.

LODGINGS—Standard motels available. Some alternatives: Bavarian Inn Lodge, alpine-inspired motel across the covered bridge from the restaurant by the same name (doubles from $99, 517/652-2651). Zehnders Bavarian Haus, new motel next to Bronner's Christmas Wonderland (doubles from $84, 517/652-6144).

CAMPING—Frankenmuth Jellystone Park Camp Resort with full hookups and an outdoor pool (517/652-6668).

DINING AND FOOD—Bavarian Inn (517/652-9941) and Zehnders of Frankenmuth (517/652-9925) for trademark chicken dinners and classic German dishes. Matterhorn Restaurant, newer establishment specializing in prime rib and barbecue (517/652-6060). Willi's Sausage Haus, 100 varieties, including low-fat blends (517/652-9041).

SHOPPING—Bronner's Christmas Wonderland, giant year-round holiday store (800/ALL-YEAR). Frankenmuth Clock Company, large selection of German cuckoo and grandfather clocks (517/652-2933). Frankenmuth Woolen Mill, high-quality sweaters and wool-filled comforters (517/652-8121). School Haus Square, 25 shops, including a Michigan products store, in a renovated elementary school (517/652-2230).

IN THE AREA—At the Outlets at Birch Run (7 miles southwest of Frankenmuth off I-75), more than 180 discount stores sell china, designer clothing, luggage and more (800/866-5900).

CELEBRATIONS—Bavarian Festival in June. Summer Music Fest in August.

INFORMATION—*Frankenmuth Chamber of Commerce Convention & Visitors Bureau, 635 S. Main St., Frankenmuth, MI 48734 (800/FUN-TOWN).* ■

MORE GREAT TOWNS

Overlooking Great Lakes waters or farther inland, these five additional towns are sure to please.

Allegan

Hills along the Kalamazoo River and nearby Lake Allegan shelter this peaceful town. Tucked into bends along the winding river, Allegan (population: 4,500) owes much to its early 1800s beginnings as a lumber center. A one-lane bridge that leads into town takes you into the old sawmill district, the downtown area and site of the community's first industry. Built in 1886, the black wrought-iron bridge hums softly as you pass over it.

On weekday guided bus tours, you'll see many early 19th-century homes just north of downtown. Pick up a map at Riverside Market along US-89 for a leisurely walk or drive on your own. The last Sunday of the month, April through September, an antiques market brings 300 dealers to the fairgrounds adjacent to downtown.

For a different view of Allegan, stroll Riverfront Plaza, a rambling flower-lined park with a boardwalk. You can stay at Winchester Inn, a brick two-story. Minnie Sophrona's specializes in home cooking. Reflections on the River serves steaks and seafood.

Location—Southwest Michigan, about 20 miles southeast of Holland.

Information—Allegan Area Chamber of Commerce, Box 338, Allegan, MI 49010 (616/673-2479).

Chesaning

Timber fortunes helped build six blocks of lavish homes along "The Boulevard," the main street in this friendly farming center. Many of the graceful Queen Annes and sprawling Prairie-style homes now hold shops crowded with crafters' works, collectibles and antiques.

The Chesaning Heritage House, a pillared white mansion transformed into a special-occasion restaurant, presides at the entrance to the historic district. Tuxedoed waiters serve savory dishes such as stuffed pork tenderloin and broiled whitefish.

Down the street, a historic old mill has been converted into Bonnymill Inn, a bed and breakfast.

The Kalamazoo River flows through Allegan.

JOHN STRAUSS

The historic fire station in downtown Manistee.

JOHN STRAUSS

More than 40,000 visitors converge on Chesaning for the weeklong Showboat Festival each July. Top performers headline shows in the riverfront park. The riverfront also hosts an arts-and-crafts fair, and crafters demonstrate their skills along The Boulevard.

Location—Central Michigan, about 20 miles west of Flint.

Information—Chesaning Chamber of Commerce, Box 83, Chesaning, MI 48616 (517/845-3055).

Manistee

The National Register of Historic Places lists the entire downtown shopping district of Manistee, located along Lake Michigan's northwest shore on the Lower Peninsula. You can ride a trolley or take a walking tour of 19th-century buildings, including the red brick First Congregational Church, the 1888 Romanesque fire station and the turn-of-the-century Ramsdell Theatre.

A new 1½ mile riverwalk links downtown and the lakeshore. Catch a fishing charter at the docks or cast your line from the piers near two public beaches.

Guests come by boat or by car to the Manistee Inn along the lakefront. The Milwaukee House specializes in Victorian atmosphere. For a special dinner, try The Glenwood (10 miles north in Onekama).

Location—Michigan's northwest Lower Peninsula, about 63 miles southwest of Traverse City.

Information—Manistee Area Chamber of Commerce, 11 Cypress St., Manistee, MI 49660 (800/288-2288).

St. Ignace

In 1671, Father Jacques Marquette built a mission at the southeast tip of Michigan's Upper Peninsula. Ever since, St. Ignace, a lively waterfront community of 2,500, has served as a gateway to rugged lands beyond.

"Big Mac," the 5-mile-long suspension bridge that connects the Upper and Lower peninsulas, dominates the skyline. Blue water surrounds the town on three sides, and wide lake views glisten from almost every street corner.

Take your time exploring shops along State Street, the main thoroughfare that parallels Lake Huron. One shop sells fudge. Paintings of Great Lakes lighthouses hang in another.

From the boardwalk that follows the lakefront for a mile, you'll see ferries headed for Mackinac Island, where Victorian-era inns and shops line the streets, and horse-drawn carriages and bicycles provide transportation (no cars allowed).

A museum at Marquette Mission Park tells about the Ojibwa, the area's earliest residents, and later the first European settlement.

Location—Southeast tip of Michigan's Upper Peninsula.

Information—St. Ignace Area Chamber of Commerce, 560 N. State St., St. Ignace, MI 49781 (800/ 338-6660).

South Haven

In summer, pleasure craft crowd the harbor at South Haven, a popular port along the southern Lake Michigan shore of Michigan's Lower Peninsula. The town's population of 6,000 swells with vacationers.

Summer visitors first arrived aboard giant steamers in the 1880s. Along North Shore Drive, three-story bed and breakfasts, including Yelton Manor, were built as inns and boardinghouses during that era.

Downtown, flower beds bloom, and shops sell everything from swimwear to collectibles. More shops and the Old Harbor Inn stand along the lakefront. Board the Idler riverboat, an old-time paddle wheeler permanently docked as a restaurant, and dine on fresh lake fish.

Across the harbor, the Michigan Maritime Museum traces the area's past, starting with the Pottawatamie.

Location—Southern Lake Michigan shore, 37 miles northwest of Kalamazoo.

Information—Lakeshore Convention & Visitors Bureau, 415 Phoenix St., South Haven, MI 49090 (800/SO-HAVEN). ■

The Idler, a floating restaurant, docks at South Haven harbor.

JOHN STRAUSS

MINNESOTA

GRAND MARAIS • LANESBORO
MANTORVILLE • NORTHFIELD
RED WING • STILLWATER • TAYLORS FALLS

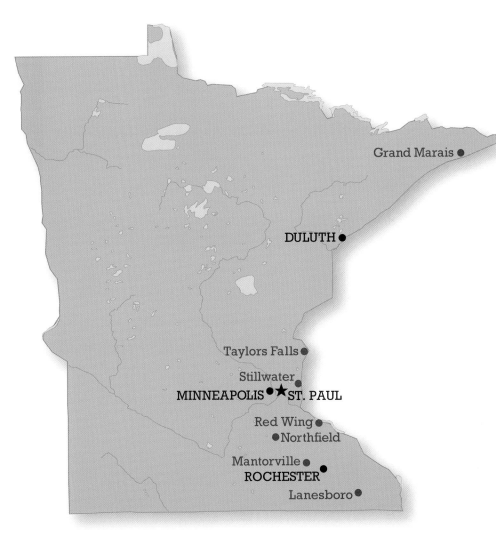

Grand Marais •

DULUTH •

Taylors Falls •

Stillwater •
MINNEAPOLIS • ★ ST. PAUL

Red Wing •
• Northfield

Mantorville •
ROCHESTER •

Lanesboro •

Small towns complement the natural wonders in this land of 10,000 lakes, north woods, lumberjacks and the call of the loon. You can visit several of Minnesota's most engaging communities in river-bluff country to the southeast. Then, journey to the north country beyond. In each of these towns, the warmth of the past lives on, enriched with modern-day comforts, sights and attractions.

For information about additional Minnesota small towns you can visit, contact: *Minnesota Office of Tourism, 500 Metro Sq., 121 Seventh Pl. E., St. Paul, MN 55101-4241 (800/657-3700).*

STILLWATER

In the 1930s, striped telephone poles guided visitors to this town, irrevocably linked to the river.

The pristine St. Croix River rushes through a craggy wooded valley separating northern Minnesota and Wisconsin. In 1843, John McKusick chose a spot along a surprisingly tranquil stretch of this swift stream to build a lumber mill. McKusick named it and the surrounding settlement Stillwater.

During the town's early days, its name must have seemed ironic. Crashing logs jammed the river, and 10 sawmills whirred along the banks. More than 50 saloons catered to rowdy loggers and mill workers. Lumber barons and merchants lavished new fortunes on handsome brick buildings downtown and mansions that crowned surrounding bluffs.

More than a century later, this community of 15,000 finally merits its peaceful name. Preservationists have rescued and restored so many of the historic buildings that the town qualifies as a living-history museum. Antiques dealers and specialty shops have nearly taken over the downtown, which parallels the river. Elaborately painted 19th-century homes—a number transformed into bed and breakfasts—decorate streets that climb a series of steep, walk-your-bike-up hills rising on the west.

Active Preservationists

Some residents say the preservation movement began in the 1960s, after a local businessman demolished Stillwater's historic depot to build a supermarket. The loss hit a civic nerve and sparked an intense save-our-heritage movement. Today, almost every structure in Stillwater gets a second life—or third or fourth.

Cub Foods, a national supermarket chain based in Stillwater, discreetly occupies a 1938 Art Deco-style school building. The usual glass-and-steel corporate tower never would have passed muster with the zoning board.

The old silver grain elevator along the river downtown was reborn as a sporting-goods store, complete with indoor mountain-climbing walls. Just north of town in the middle of a county park, the Georgian-style building that once was the poor farm has been transformed into Outing Lodge at Pine Point. In a structure dating to 1858, this soothing retreat features a massive fireplace, plus floors and paneling of golden pine.

Along Main Street, historic buildings house tiny shops and restaurants. Like movie sets, the storefronts can fool first-time visitors. The Grand Garage, formerly the old Stillwater Motor Company, harbors a dessert theater. Some of the 20 stores sell everything from Guatemalan imports to custom bronzes and Irish woolens and memorabilia.

At the north end of Main Street, the old tin-sided Staples Mill appears to house just four stores, including a tasting room for Northern Vineyards, a local winery. But when you climb the stairs, you'll discover nearly 80 antiques dealers tucked away among the mill's upper levels, like treasures in Grandma's attic.

The trendy flavor of the Twin Cities (just 20 miles east) also has nudged its way onto Main Street in the form of bistros, espresso bars, and parlors serving mango-ginger ice cream.

Lumber's Legacy

Along the hilly, tree-lined streets that climb from downtown, Stillwater's founders built stone churches and pine homes similar to the ones that they'd known back East.

Nineteenth-century churches with tall spires still hold Sunday services. The town's original Italianate courthouse, built in 1867 and open for tours, contains the local Red Cross chapter. You'll probably see at least one example of nearly every architectural style you can imagine: Queen Anne, Italianate, Classic Revival, French Second Empire, Greek Revival and neo-Romanesque. Most structures have been perfectly restored and bright-

Cruise boats have replaced the logs that once jammed the Stillwater riverfront.

ly painted in spirited color schemes.

Innkeepers have restored eight of Stillwater's grand homes as bed and breakfasts. A number have been refurbished so carefully that they feel more like museums.

Lumber baron William Sauntry built one of the most extravagant mansions. His 25-room Queen Anne contained 10 fireplaces and an adjoining Moorish gymnasium with mirrored ballroom, reflecting pool, bowling alley and tennis court. The gym has been converted into apartments, but the house survives as a bed and breakfast. The Sauntry Mansion also features original canvas painted ceilings and period furniture.

"We're preservationists who opened a bed and breakfast," says one innkeeper, succinctly capturing the Stillwater attitude.

White-Pine Wealth

At times during Stillwater's early days, the St. Croix seemed like an immense beaver dam. Log jams were so dense, you could walk across the river without getting your feet wet. Sometimes, the river's flow was blocked for weeks— once as long as 57 days! The Stillwater Depot, Logging and Railroad Museum downtown tells the story of the community's early, wilder days.

Built to resemble a 19th-century train station, with high wooden ceilings and long benches, the depot building also is a departure point for the *Minnesota Zephyr,* a 1940s train that offers dinner rides. During the trip, you enjoy five-course meals served on crisp white linen.

Inside the station, blow-ups of old black-and-white photos show the town at the height of the logging era. One startling picture captures a man in coveralls, standing atop a pile of logs as high as a house.

In 1848, Wisconsin became the 30th state. The next year, Congress formed an official Minnesota Territory. Stillwater thought it had a shot at becoming the capital, but St. Paul prevailed. As a consolation prize, Stillwater won a territorial prison.

Staples Mill, anchoring Main Street, houses antiques shops and other stores.

Prison jobs thrilled residents of the town, since years of cutting without planting had almost entirely depleted the area's pine forests.

Changing Fortunes

The last log floated down the St. Croix in 1914. As part of the tour aboard the red trolley that ferries visitors around town, guide Robert Raleigh recounts Stillwater's decline.

"The town was left choking on its own sawdust," he declares.

By 1930, Stillwater's population had dwindled by more than half. Soon after that, Arthur and Nelle Palmer retired to Stillwater from their vaudeville touring days and bought the Lowell Inn. The brick replica of George Washington's Mount Vernon still presides along Second Street.

Arthur knew that if the town were to prosper, he needed visitors from the Twin Cities. He painted blue-and-white stripes on the telephone poles along the road that led to Minneapolis. Then, he paid for big newspaper ads urging people to follow the poles. Visitors have been coming ever since.

Yet, despite all the newcomers, Stillwater retains the character of a small town. Summer concerts in the amphitheater in Pioneer Park, a hilltop preserve that overlooks Stillwater and the St. Croix River, always attract friendly crowds. Residents share jugs of iced tea while listening to the music. Even if you're just visiting for a day or two, you're sure to feel at home.

By Ad Hudler.

TRAVEL GUIDE

LOCATION—Eastern Minnesota, 20 miles east of the Twin Cities.

LODGINGS—Standard motels available on the newer west side of town. Some alternatives: The Outing Lodge at Pine Point north of Stillwater, in the middle of a park (doubles from $99, suites from $115, 612/439-9747). The William Sauntry Mansion, six rooms in a late Victorian home (doubles from $89, 800/828-2653). James A. Mulvey Residence Inn, five rooms, one with two claw-foot side-by-side bathtubs. Breakfast in an enclosed sunny porch (doubles from $99, 612/430-8008).

DINING AND FOOD—Brine's Bar & Restaurant for home-style sausages and sandwiches, including one of the region's best hamburgers, served on home-baked buns (612/439-7556). Savories European Bistro Cafe, changing innovative menu of salads and pasta dishes, as well as homemade desserts (612/430-0702). Dock Cafe, riverside outdoor dining (612/430-3770).

CAMPING—William O'Brien State Park (about 14 miles north of Stillwater), river access, as well as canoe rentals, miles of hiking and cross-country trails and an interpretive nature center (612/433-0500).

SHOPPING—Tamarack House Gallery, contemporary works from Midwest artists, including many sculptures (612/439-9393). Kmitsch Girls, a toy store from yesteryear with a huge doll selection (612/430-1827). Architectural Antiques, pieces such as mantels and light fixtures salvaged from old buildings (612/439-2133).

IN THE AREA—At Minnesota Interstate State Park (about 30 miles north of Stillwater), you can climb a path that leads to the top of towering cliffs and view the St. Croix River rushing down a deep, narrow gorge known as The Dalles. Boat excursions are available.

CELEBRATIONS—Rivertown Art Fair in May. Lumberjack Days in July. Art & Jazz Festival in October. Victorian Christmas Celebration from November until Christmas.

INFORMATION—*Stillwater Area Chamber of Commerce, Brick Alley Bldg., 423 S. Main St., Stillwater, MN 55082 (612/439-7700).* ■

GRAND MARAIS

With Lake Superior in its front yard and the north woods at its back door, this town's scenery is tops.

The timeworn ridges of the Sawtooth Mountains nearly encircle Grand Marais, a onetime fishing village that frames a natural harbor along Minnesota's Lake Superior shore. Though the fur-trading voyageurs first ventured here almost 3 centuries ago, this town still claims just a speck of land at the edge of the giant inland sea. From the town limits, a wilderness sprawls for 10,000 square miles across Minnesota's northeast corner.

In the small business district, galleries selling local artists' works and gift shops mix with stores stocking heavy-duty gear for fishing, canoeing the area's pristine granite-bottom lakes and trekking through the surrounding north woods.

Once primarily a way station, this town of 1,100 has attracted a loyal following. Motels rim a section of shore, and little cabin complexes scatter along surrounding streets. An artists' colony also thrives here, dedicated to capturing the area's wild beauty.

Traffic-Stopping Vista

US-61 follows the lakeshore for 110 miles from Duluth north to Grand Marais. At the southwest edge of town, the smooth blacktop swoops into the business district from the shoulders of the Sawtooth Range, remnants of prehistoric volcanoes.

Below, Grand Marais surrounds a harbor bobbing with sailboats and sport-fishing cruisers. Vast Lake Superior, which stretches to the horizon, laps at the town with white-tipped indigo waves. You'll be tempted to stop at the park along the harbor. Children line up to have their pictures taken beside the park's centerpiece, a tall sculpture of two bear cubs climbing a tree.

During most summer days, Lake Superior splashes almost playfully around the breakwater that protects the harbor and lighthouse at its tip. It's hard to imagine the furious November gales that hurl crashing waves almost over the top of the tower.

When the lake is calm, you can follow a walkway that takes you across the breakwater to the light tower. From that angle, with the woodsy bluffs looming overhead, Grand Marais looks even smaller still.

On the warmest days (80 degrees is considered sweltering here), breezes blow in occasional chilly puffs, reminding you that soaring blue skies and calm waters won't last. Perhaps that's why a seize-the-moment camaraderie infects visitors and locals alike.

Fishing Poles And Paintings

The compact business district follows the harbor. Squawking gulls waddle beside vacationers, who stroll among the shops in converted cottages and a hodgepodge of storefronts.

The Lake Superior Trading Post, a two-story cedar emporium beside the harbor, stocks quality merchandise that ranges from fishing lures and backpacks to hand-woven rugs and collectible Christmas ornaments. You'll also see an assortment of coats, boots and caps, reminders of how cold winters get this far north.

Northern Impulses brims with birchbark baskets, handcrafted jewelry and fragrant candles. Merchandise of every sort packs narrow aisles and towering shelves at Joyne's Department Store & Ben Franklin. You can buy mosquito repellent, a lumberjack hat complete with ear flaps or a souvenir sweatshirt.

A fierce-looking three-dimensional giant fish leers from the roof of The Beaver House. Inside the store, you'll see racks and bins of bright-colored lures, bobbers and other fishing supplies. Clerks gladly point novices to the neon-hued spinners that walleyes seem to love or the lures that giant lake trout are biting on that day.

Viking Hus, at the edge of the business district along US-61, celebrates the area's Scandinavian heritage with

LAYNE KENNEDY

In summer, Lake Superior appears deceptively placid along the harbor.

imports from the lands the Vikings visited. Shelves hold delicate teacups from Russia, intricate silver jewelry from Sweden and devilish-looking trolls from Norway.

Nearby restaurants tempt you with hearty fare and mesmerizing views. You can munch on grilled burgers and sample from-scratch pie on the Upper Deck at the Blue Water Cafe, a casual local favorite beside the harbor.

Built by a lumber baron, a log mansion along US-61 on the town's southwest edge houses Birch Terrace. This cozy eatery specializes in fresh lake trout and barbecued ribs.

Artists' Outpost
Even before the first all-weather road reached Grand Marais in the 1920s, artists traveled here to paint the area's dramatic north-woods landscapes. Today, about 50 artists live and work in the Grand Marais vicinity year-round. During summer, the number swells to more than 200.

One of the area's first and best-known artists came to the tiny village as a bride. Near the turn of the century, the owner of the fur-trading post overlooking the harbor wooed Anna C. Johnson, a Swedish girl from Manistee, Michigan.

Anna had studied art at an Illinois college. In Grand Marais, she continued to paint, capturing her neighbors and local scenes in softly brushed oils. Her paintings hang in the Johnson Heritage Post Gallery, a new log structure donated by the Johnsons' son on the site of the original fur-trading post.

Another of the area's renowned artists, Birney Quick, started coming to the North Shore to fish. In 1947, he founded the Grand Marais Art Colony as a branch of the Minneapolis School of Art. The nonprofit organization now holds children's classes and summer workshops for artists and writers.

Artworks fill local establishments such as the Sivertson Gallery. In this converted cottage, paintings of Lake Superior roiling in the winter storms share the walls with impressionistic renderings of the surrounding forests, glistening with autumn color.

Dine on traditional favorites at the Birch Terrace restaurant.

LAYNE KENNEDY

Into the Woods

The Gunflint Trail, a 53-mile-long two-lane, angles north and west from the edge of Grand Marais, bound for the vast Superior National Forest. This former logging track leads to more than a dozen small resorts and the Boundary Waters Canoe Area, a network of lakes and streams that's off-limits to motorized craft.

Steps from the business district, Lake Superior rushes against beaches piled with water-smoothed stones. Forests of pines, birches and maples crowd the edge of town, as if poised to reclaim this small patch of civilization.

Some of the area's most scenic trails start right in town. You can follow an easy 1-mile path to Sweetheart's Bluff, an overlook with a panoramic view of the harbor and Grand Marais.

Generations of painters have set up their easels here, but it also makes the perfect spot for a quiet picnic. In the distance, the deep-blue lake melds with the sky and a 1,000-foot freighter inches along the horizon.

By Barbara Morrow.

TRAVEL GUIDE

LOCATION—Along the Lake Superior shore in northeast Minnesota, about 110 miles northeast of Duluth.

LODGINGS—Standard motels available. Some favorite alternatives: Best Western Superior Inn & Suites, all rooms with lake views (doubles from $90, 800/842-VIEW). East Bay Hotel along the lakeshore downtown, from bargain-priced economy rooms to newly decorated suites (doubles from $38, 800/414-2807). The Shoreline, motel overlooking Lake Superior at the edge of downtown (doubles from $74, 800/247-6020). Naniboujou Lodge, a beautifully refurbished 1920s hunting lodge, now an inn (15 miles north of town along the lake, doubles from $69, 218/387-2688).

CAMPING—Grand Marais Municipal Campground, more than 300 tent and RV sites with hookups near the shore and downtown (218/387-1712).

DINING AND FOOD—Angry Trout Cafe, grilled lake trout on the waterfront (218/387-1265). Birch Terrace, Lake Superior fish, steaks and ribs in a log mansion overlooking the shore (218/387-2215). Blue Water Cafe, casual eatery downtown, serving breakfast all day, plus burgers and home-style pies (218/387-1597). Sven & Ole's, sandwiches and pizza, thin or thick crust, topped with fresh ingredients (218/387-1713). World's Best Donuts, light, freshly baked treats in an apple-red cottage downtown (218/387-1345). The dining room at Naniboujou Lodge (see Lodgings), decorated with striking Native American-inspired designs (218/387-2688).

SHOPPING—Lake Superior Trading Post, assortment of gifts and north-woods gear (218/387-2020). Sivertson Gallery, local artists' works in a lakeside cottage downtown (218/387-2491). Viking Hus, Scandinavian and European imports (218/387-2589).

IN THE AREA—The National Park Service has re-created a late 1700s fur trading depot at Grand Portage National Monument (36 miles north of Grand Marais, 218/475-2202). From Grand Portage, a ferry travels to Isle Royale National Park, an island wilderness 20 miles offshore in Lake Superior (Grand Portage-Isle Royale Transportation Line, 715/392-2100). Nearby, at Grand Portage State Park, opened in 1994, trails lead to Minnesota's highest waterfall along the Pigeon River.

CELEBRATIONS—Annual Arts Festival in July. Fishermen's Picnic in August. Winterfest in January.

INFORMATION—*Grand Marais Chamber of Commerce, Box 1048, Grand Marais, MN 55604 (888/922-5000).* ■

LANESBORO

From railways to bikeways, this history-rich town thrives today, as it did in the 1870s.

As lazy as a summer afternoon, the Root River meanders through southeast Minnesota's towering bluffs. The town of Lanesboro hugs the banks of the river in the shadows of a 300-foot forested ridge.

During the last century, the coming of the railroad brought prosperity and what seemed to be a promise of unlimited growth to this town of about 900. Entrepreneurs considered the new rail stop a sure bet to become Minnesota's next boomtown.

But today, you'd never guess that Lanesboro's citizens once harbored hopes of their town developing into a thriving commercial center. Restored 19th-century storefronts, many housing little shops selling gifts and antiques, line the broad main street. A number of the homes that the town's early notables built now open their doors to travelers as bed and breakfasts. A paved state bicycle trail has replaced the old rail line, cutting through the center of town.

The closest Lanesboro comes to bustling these days is on mild summer afternoons when steady streams of bicyclists and walkers arrive to explore the state trail. Without concern for traffic, riders pedal leisurely through the middle of town.

High Hopes Fulfilled

Though the trains stopped running in 1973, the railroad's legacy helped spark Lanesboro's rebirth. The state acquired the old railbed for the 36-mile-long bicycle trail. That path, in turn, brought visitors and new businesses to the community.

Visitors loved downtown Lanesboro's ornate facades and opulent, if somewhat neglected, Victorian homes. This newfound interest in the houses around town gave residents new ideas. They began seeing their community from a historic perspective. A preservation society formed, worked hard and eventually succeeded in getting downtown Lanesboro listed in the National Register of Historic Places.

A decade later, business owners have restored most of the downtown. A one-time general store houses Cornucopia, a gallery of 50 regional artists' works. The historic creamery building is home to the Scenic Valley Winery. Capron Hardware, which still sells tools and plumbing supplies, also rents bikes that line up out front. Down the street, the Commonweal Theater Company stages productions in a renovated silent-movie house.

A shop called Down Home occupies the 1890 general store. The shelves hold vintage linens, interesting odds and ends from local farm sales, collectible glassware and teddy bears.

Owner Linda Hazel says the old general-store building once stood on the corner. But the bank wanted to build on that site, so the store was hoisted onto rollers and moved inch by inch to the adjacent lot.

"Believe it or not," Linda says with a laugh, "the general store stayed open for business the whole time."

Music in the Streets

Polka music spills onto the street from Das Wurst House, an old-fashioned sandwich shop. After filling visitors with frothy homemade root beer, hunks of from-scratch sausage and warm pumpernickel bread, owners Arv and Jan Fabian strike up the Das Wurst House band. Arv, who used to run an auto-repair operation from the back of the shop, pumps an ornate concertina, and Jan plays the piano behind the counter.

A rectangular stone building nearby, once an 1800s undertaker's parlor, houses Mrs. B's Historic Lanesboro Inn. Guests settle into 10 rooms decorated with antiques and locally made furnishings and quilts. Fruits and vegetables from the inn's garden star in inventive, mouthwatering dishes served in the lower-level restaurant.

PERRY STRUSE

Bicyclists of all ages pedal the Root River Trail from Lanesboro.

In 1890, Michael Scanlan, banker and Lanesboro's founder, lavished his wealth on a nine-room Queen Anne home. At the Scanlan House, now a bed and breakfast with five guest rooms, you can bask once again in graceful, Victorian-style elegance.

The state trail attracted Twin Cities lawyer Peggy Addicks to Lanesboro. The gracious old homes and friendly atmosphere convinced her to stay. "It was like walking into a storybook," Peggy recalls. Now, she welcomes guests to the Cady Hayes House Bed & Breakfast, a Queen Anne named for the bachelor farmer who built it in 1893.

Along the Trail

The Root River Trail wanders for 53 miles over creaky trestles and through corridors of limestone beginning at the trailhead 25 miles east near Rushford. State-16 follows roughly the same route. Along the way, the path crosses 48 old railroad bridges, some as long as 500 feet. It also travels through dense woodlands, where you might see deer bounding through the trees or hawks soaring overhead.

The broad trail accommodates all sorts of traffic. Walkers stroll for a mile or two and then head back to town. Families steer fat-tired bikes, often slowly enough so the littlest member can keep up on a training-wheeler. Serious cyclists, resplendent in neon-hued gear, zip past, delighted to ride without dodging cars. Inline skaters chat as they glide along.

You can travel all the way to Rushford's 1867 depot or ride only as far as the tiny community of Whalan

Fall color tints Lanesboro and the surrounding countryside.

LAYNE KENNEDY

Stay at the Cady Hayes House, a Lanesboro bed and breakfast.

PERRY STRUSE

(population: 95) 5 miles east. The Overland Inn, Whalan's casual hometown cafe, bakes 160 pies a week. Hungry pedalers stop for fat slabs of the inn's special-recipe apple caramel.

The trail stays open year-round, though summer probably brings the most traffic. When snow blankets the valley, cross-country skiers and snowmobilers share the path.

You also can canoe the Root River. It's pure pleasure to paddle and drift along with the lazy current on an all-day outing. Along the way, you might see anglers casting for plump trout.

The Railroad Days

The Lanesboro Historic Museum, in a handsomely restored storefront on the east end of downtown, documents Lanesboro's early days.

By January 1867, the tracks for the Southern Minnesota line extended as far west as Rushford. Officials of the railroad were searching for the best route through the steep-sided valley to the level plains beyond. A mostly unsettled spot in a crook of the Root River between Rushford and Preston seemed the ideal location for a dam and a depot.

Within a couple of years, Lanesboro sprang to life. The Phoenix Hotel, a three-story limestone structure that cost the princely sum of $50,000 to build, was hailed as the finest in the West. Newcomers constructed more hotels and rooming houses, restaurants and stores. Lanesboro became a major staging area for Norwegians heading west to North Dakota and South Dakota, and the population swelled to around 2,000.

Legend has it that "Buffalo Bill" Cody performed his first Wild West Show in Lanesboro with the help of the local Winnebagos. One museum photo shows a gun that Cody presented to Dr. David Powell, the town physician, who was a comrade of Cody during the Civil War.

Changing Times

With completion of the dam and the availability of abundant water power, Lanesboro shifted to industry for growth. Within a few years, four flour mills rose on the riverbanks. Leaders had hoped to bring factories.

Since the west was mostly settled, the flood of immigrants slowed to a trickle. Merchants missed the money that the newcomers spent on equipment and supplies. In 1885, fire destroyed the Phoenix Hotel, one of the town's biggest attractions.

All but one of the flour mills also burned. But by then, years of wheat growing had sapped the area's soil, and farmers turned to raising livestock. With its proud downtown buildings and grand homes, Lanesboro grudgingly settled into life as a sleepy agricultural center.

Ironically, Lanesboro's fall from boomtown status undoubtedly saved old buildings and homes that might have been torn down. Now, guests at the Cady Hayes House remark about the town's storybook quality.

"Lanesboro is very much a real place," innkeeper Peggy Addicks maintains. "But we've managed to hold onto what a lot of other small towns have lost."

By Barbara Morrow.

TRAVEL GUIDE

LOCATION—Southeast Minnesota, about 125 miles southeast of the Twin Cities.

LODGINGS—Mrs. B's Historic Lanesboro Inn & Restaurant, 10 plush rooms in a history-rich downtown building (doubles from $50, 800/657-4710). Cady Hayes House, three guest rooms in a restored Queen Anne (doubles from $75, 507/467-2621). Green Gables Inn, new locally owned motel with 12 rooms (doubles from $55, 507/467-2936). Historic Scanlan House, a five-room bed and breakfast in an 1889 Victorian home (doubles from $65, 800/944-2158).

CAMPING—Sylvan Park Campground, 100 sites, including 40 with hookups, in the park at the center of town. Old Barn Resort (7 miles west near Preston), 162 sites, 127 with hookups (507/467-2512).

DINING AND FOOD—Das Wurst House, homemade sausage, root beer and German music (507/467-2902). Mrs. B's Historic Lanesboro Inn (see Lodgings), inventive fare featuring fresh ingredients in the bed and breakfast's lower-level dining room

(800/657-4710). River Valley Cheese, to watch cheese made in the mornings with milk from the area's Amish farms (507/467-7000). White Front Cafe, casual, economical eatery with daily breakfast and lunch specials (507/467-3747).

SHOPPING—Cornucopia Art Center, nonprofit gallery in a onetime general store showcasing paintings, sculptures and other works of regional artists (507/467-2446). Down Home, gifts and antiques in a historic building (507/467-2555).

IN THE AREA—The Root River Trail, 53-mile paved former railbed, popular with bicyclers and hikers, passes through Lanesboro. Pick up information and maps at the trail center in Lanesboro (507/467-2552). Capron Hardware in Lanesboro rents bikes (800/726-5030). You also can paddle the easygoing Root River (Lanesboro Canoe Rental, 507/467-2948).

INFORMATION—Lanesboro Visitors Center, 206 Parkway N., Box 20, Lanesboro, MN 55949 (800/944-2670). ∎

MORE GREAT TOWNS

Pastoral scenes and pristine rivers backdrop many of the state's charming small towns.

Mantorville

Today, the population of Mantorville hovers around 900. But once, this southern Minnesota town was a key way station for travelers headed west.

Downtown, 1860s limestone buildings, all listed in the National Register of Historic Places, line the main street. A walking-tour map takes you to sites such as the Restoration House, an 1856 home and adjacent pioneer log cabin, and the 1871 Dodge County Courthouse, Minnesota's oldest courthouse still in use. You also can climb into a horse-drawn buggy for a tour.

The Grand Old Mansion, an opulent 1899 home, opens its doors for tours and as a bed and breakfast. Stop for lunch or dinner at the Hubbell House. The mid-1800s hotel has been transformed into an antique-filled restaurant specializing in onion rings, steaks and broiled walleye. Save room for the ice cream pie; it's extra rich with chocolate, caramel and pecans.

Location—Southern Minnesota, about 15 miles west of Rochester.

Information—Mantorville Chamber of Commerce, Mantorville, MN 55955 (507/635-3231).

Northfield

Northfield gained a reputation as the site of a bank robbery that Jesse James bungled. But this inviting community of 15,000 alongside the Cannon River

The 19th-century Archer House stars in downtown Northfield.

LAYNE KENNEDY

attracts more people than just curious history buffs.

Nationally known Carleton and St. Olaf colleges, friendly rivals, welcome visitors to their manicured campuses. Stroll through Carleton's 400-acre arboretum, overlooking the rolling river valley. On homecoming weekends, downtown explodes in school colors: blue and yellow for Carleton students, black and gold for "Oles."

Shoppers and architecture buffs browse downtown's Riverside Commons, which bustles with specialty shops, antiques stores and boutiques. Renovated 19th-century buildings line Division Street, including the red brick Archer House, a restored turn-of-the-century hotel with 38 comfortable guest rooms.

Farther south along Division, you can visit the Scriver Building, former site of the First National Bank and Jesse James' attempted holdup. Each September for the Defeat of Jesse James Days festival, interpreters re-enact the robbery and are foiled again.

Near the St. Olaf's campus, The Ole Store and Cafe, one of Northfield's longest-standing restaurants, serves hearty soups and sandwiches, along with its renowned Ole Rolls (gooey cinnamon buns).

Location—Southern Minnesota, 30 miles south of the Twin Cities.

Information—Northfield Area Chamber of Commerce, 500 Water St. S., Box 198, Northfield, MN 55057-0198 (800/658-2548).

Red Wing

Like the back of a giant elephant, Barn Bluff looms over downtown Red Wing, cradled between towering ridges and the Mississippi River southeast of the Twin Cities.

In the 1800s, this community of 15,000 thrived on grain, pottery and shoemaking. Restored brick buildings dating to that era line Main Street. Many of the structures now house shops and restaurants.

The St. James Hotel, a handsome red brick landmark trimmed in white, spans most of a city block. Wheat barons built the hotel in 1873 to offer some of the poshest lodgings along the river. Antiques and reproductions decorate the 60 renovated rooms. Dine at the St. James or Liberty's Restaurant and Lounge, a casual eatery decorated with photos of Red Wing's past.

Down the street, T.B. Sheldon Memorial Auditorium, a renovated 1904 playhouse, hosts performances once again. On the west edge of town, the cavernous factory that produced Red Wing Pottery is now an outlet mall, housing more than 50 discount and antiques shops. Some dealers stock the pottery's original crocks, stamped with the trademark red bird's wing.

Location—Southern Minnesota, about 45 miles southeast of the Twin Cities.

Information—Red Wing Visitors & Convention Bureau, 418 Levee St., Red Wing, MN 55066 (800/498-3444).

Taylors Falls

Around Taylors Falls, rolling woodlands spill into the glacier-carved valley of the St. Croix River, which forms the boundary between northern Minnesota and Wisconsin. Originally a fur trading post that the French established, this community of 700 traces its heritage to the New Englanders who settled here in the 1800s. Today, the town is a gateway to the upper St. Croix River Valley.

During the last century, Taylors Falls was a logging and steamboating center. Many buildings date to that time. Most historic homes cluster along Bench and River streets and in the Angel Hill Historic District. You can tour the W.H.C. Folsom House, a Greek Revival built in 1855. The Chisago House features bountiful buffets (Fridays–Sundays).

Board a double-decked paddle wheeler for cruises to stretches of the river where startling rock formations tower above the water. Nearby, Interstate State Park encompasses some of the river valley's most rugged and beautiful scenery.

Location—Eastern Minnesota, 45 miles northeast of the Twin Cities.

Information—Taylors Falls Chamber of Commerce, 333 Bench St., Taylors Falls, MN 55084 (612/465-6661). ■

MISSOURI

ARROW ROCK • CARTHAGE • HANNIBAL HERMANN • KIMMSWICK • ST. CHARLES STE. GENEVIEVE • WESTON

If there are rewards for taking the roads less traveled, you're sure to discover them in the Show Me State. In Missouri, which flavors its Midwest character with a southern accent, an abundance of small towns dot the banks of the Mississippi and Missouri rivers. The American frontier had its beginnings in Missouri's early trail stops, many of which retain their homespun charm. Farther south, friendly hill towns welcome visitors amid the forests, lakes and timeworn Ozark Mountains.

For information about additional Missouri small towns you can visit, contact: *Missouri Div. of Tourism, Truman State Office Bldg., Box 1055, Jefferson City, MO 65102 (573/751-4133).*

WESTON

Choose pure serenity or sightseeing and shopping in this town that the Missouri River sidestepped.

Brick storefronts from the 19th century line Weston's Main Street, and bright-red benches invite you to linger awhile. Unhurried shopkeepers chat amid rainbows of Depression glass, cadres of handcrafted Santas and neatly folded stacks of turn-of-the-century linens. On downtown's busiest corner, a boy and his dad ponder a game on a hand-painted checkerboard.

Residents call Weston, located just east of the Missouri River in the Show Me State's northwest corner, the town that time forgot. But on sunny summer afternoons, this also is a place where you can forget about time.

"It's great to slow down," says Lynn Wylie, in town from Kansas City, just a half-hour south. "Weston really makes you forget about thinking you have to make every second count."

This town attracts antiques lovers, who browse and buy at dozens of shops and specialty stores; artists, who gain inspiration from the historic buildings and peaceful setting; and sightseers, eager to visit an outlet for one of the nation's oldest distilleries based here and tour Weston Vineyards. But you don't need to visit Weston with a particular purpose in mind. You simply can relax, enjoy yourself and while away a couple of days or an afternoon.

Meandering Along Main Street

Weston took its name from its location, once the nation's westernmost trading post. The town was born in 1837 as part of the Platte Purchase, which opened 2 million acres to settlers. Weston boomed as a river port, thanks to steamboat traffic that churned up the Missouri River from New Orleans and Natchez, Mississippi. By 1853, the population had swelled to 5,000, rivaling St. Louis, and Weston became Missouri's second-largest port.

Massive floods more than 100 years ago caused the Missouri to change course, leaving Weston high and dry.

But this town of 1,500 has retained much of the flavor of an early 19th-century Missouri River port. More than 200 of Weston's buildings, many beautifully refurbished, date to those days.

A hint of southern charm persists in the architecture of the vintage storefronts and homes along Main and surrounding streets. Antiques shops, art galleries and specialty stores pack the four-block shopping district.

One of three J.P.'s Antiques shops specializes in Depression-era glassware. Vintage furniture and more glassware pack Main Street Galleria. Handcrafted Santas, storybook-character accessories, candles and other decorations fill Kriss Kringle's. Plum Pudding, a shop and tearoom, stocks gifts and Victorian-era clothing.

Near the historic district, the acclaimed America Bowman Restaurant serves hearty homemade fare on the site of the oldest brewery west of New York state's Hudson River. Be sure to try the Missouri ham sandwiches on sweet-potato scones.

After a 100-Year Slumber

During Weston's boom, steamboats jammed the river, and wagon trains lined the waterfront, loading supplies for destinations west. Businesses, from flour mills to brewing companies, flourished. Prosperous residents built eight churches, private schools and stately Federal-style homes like those they'd left behind in the South.

But by 1880, two fires had gutted Weston's business district. The river had flooded five times, finally setting its course 2 miles away. Within 10 years, Weston's population dwindled to only 1,000 residents.

For almost 100 years, Weston remained virtually untouched. Then, in the 1960s, interest in historical preservation reawakened this sleepy town. The historic district now encompasses 22 blocks.

Along streets shaded by towering

Antiques and specialty shops line Weston's business district.

HOTEL WESTON

oaks and maples, you see impeccably restored antebellum cottages that remind you of the Old South. They stand alongside gaily painted Victorians that are trimmed with quirky gingerbread details and curlicues.

Five historic buildings house bed and breakfasts. The Benner House, as fancy as an old-time riverboat with its "steamboat Gothic" trim, pampers overnight guests with shiny brass beds and claw-foot tubs.

History Distilled

Many of Weston's settlers hailed from Kentucky, Tennessee and Virginia, bringing with them their tobacco, whiskey and wine industries. Today, the town continues to capitalize on that southern heritage.

In fact, you can wake up at the Inn at Weston Landing on the site of the Old Royal Brewery, shop for antiques in a turn-of-the-century tobacco barn and dine at The Vineyards, a restaurant in an antebellum cottage.

Visitors can tour Pirtle's Winery, which is located in a 130-year-old former Evangelical Lutheran church. Pirtle's mead, a honey wine, is one of its most popular.

In 1856, Ben Holladay founded McCormick Distilling Company in Weston. Today, McCormick is the oldest continuously operating distillery on its original site in the nation. Adults can sample "the whiskey that opened the West" along with the distillery's other products at the McCormick Country Store on Main Street.

The shop also sells souvenirs from T-shirts to cocktail glasses. Pick up an information sheet that tells McComick's history. Clerks are glad to

Benner House, one of four bed and breakfasts.

BOB BARRETT

explain how aging in charred oak casks transforms newly distilled "white lightning" into mellow bourbon.

Roots That Run Deep

"There's a story behind everything," says Etta Marie Brill, who's the curator of the Weston Historical Museum. You'll get a glimpse of the town's saga amid the museum's Battenburg lace table cover, a square 1864 Steinway piano, Civil War weapons and old wheelwright's tools.

A World War I Red Cross fundraising quilt, complete with the embroidered signature of President Woodrow Wilson, hangs near the marriage certificates and a yellowing dress used for christening five generations of one family. In Weston, Etta Marie explains, families have roots.

"My husband's family has been in this town for four generations," she says. "I'm a newcomer. I've just been here 50 years."

So deep are these ties that a few of Weston's historic homes have been occupied by members of the same family since the 1860s. For instance, the descendants of legendary frontiersman Daniel Boone lived in the Price-Loyles House, around the corner from the museum, from 1864 to 1989.

Now, visitors can tour that three-story Federal-style mansion, filled with four generations of family heirlooms. Guests marvel at antique furnishings and keepsakes such as glittery hat pins, lacy valentines, and evening slippers the size of a child's hand. You'll see tobacco plugs braided into decorative shapes, delicate ladies' spittoons and even opium pipes (anesthesia used by a dentist who once lived here).

Guide Frances Feldhausen points out a rosewood piano with cast-iron legs. According to family lore, the piano was so heavy that it took six strong men to carry it from the waterfront into the parlor in the late 1860s.

The piano has stayed there ever since—not so unusual for Weston. Times change, it seems, but much of this old Missouri River port remains fixed in the last century.

By Ann Wylie.

STE. GENEVIEVE

Whether it's French or German heritage you're seeking, you'll relish Missouri's oldest town.

A sign at the city limits proudly welcomes you to Ste. Genevieve, founded in 1735. On the outskirts of this southeast Missouri community of 4,400, you'd never guess it's Missouri's oldest town, settled by French farmers and traders decades before the U.S. was born. But as you head into the business district, you begin to notice signs of Ste. Genevieve's heritage.

History has a way of flickering to life in this river town. That's partly because some of North America's oldest buildings survive here. Several have been restored and are preserved as historic sites you can tour.

Guides tell the stories of people who lived and worked here more than two centuries ago. Their accounts include such detail that you may learn more about the town's early citizens than you know about your neighbors at home.

Authentic French Flair

The old downtown centers on the courthouse square. The Gothic spire of Ste. Genevieve Catholic Church towers over one side of the square. The Southern Hotel, a three-story Federal-style masterpiece, presides grandly nearby.

On another corner, the Old Brick House, a casual restaurant known for its fried chicken and huge buffets, occupies the oldest brick building west of the Mississippi.

Narrow streets that seem more suited to carts and carriages than to cars thread through the surrounding historic district. You'll see lacy wrought-iron fences, French Colonial-style homes with wide porches called galleries, and sturdy brick buildings that German settlers constructed when they arrived during the mid-1800s.

Stop first at the tourist information center along Main Street, which bounds the east edge of the downtown historic district. A film and exhibits tell Ste. Genevieve's story.

French farmers first settled on rich bottomland, 3 miles south of the town's present site. In 1785, a devastating flood forced the community to seek higher ground.

More than 30 buildings from that era and the early 1800s survive. The rising river still threatens periodically, but heroic sandbagging has preserved the historic district. Many of the old buildings still house families and businesses. At the visitors center, pick up a walking-tour map that points out historic structures and takes you to nearby buildings you can tour.

Inviting Homes to View

Even more than two centuries after he built it, Louis Bolduc's house along what is now Main Street hints at the trader's wealth and position. The French Colonial-style house has been meticulously restored as a historic site and furnished with some original and other authentic pieces. You almost expect the well-to-do family to return home at any moment.

On the outside, you can see the massive oak timbers lined up vertically and mortared with a mixture of clay and straw. The posts rest on a stone foundation and support a peaked roof that slopes downward, shading the gallery. Inside, plaster (a rarity on the frontier) covers the walls of two airy, high-ceilinged rooms, separated by a wide center hall.

Volunteer guide Shirley Myers points to furnishings that also would have set the Bolducs apart from their neighbors: a massive armoire, which still bears a water mark from the 1785 flood; an ornately carved *pantier* (bread cooler); and curtains of printed fabric, some of the first of its kind, hanging at the windows.

Dark wood dining chairs look child-size. "These are full-size chairs," Shirley tells the group. "The average Frenchman in Bolduc's day was less than 5 feet tall."

An herb garden like the one the Bolducs probably planted 200 years ago flourishes behind the house. Scents

FRANK OBERLE

The Bolduc House in Ste. Genevieve dates back to the early 1700s.

saturate the still, warm air: soapy box-wood, sweet rose geranium and pungent mint. Visitors retreat to the shade of the gallery, a wraparound porch that helped keep the French settlers' homes cool.

The house next door, built in 1820 for Bolduc's granddaughter, shows signs of Ste. Genevieve's American-ization. Polished pine floors and fur-nishings such as a curved horsehair sofa and ornate English dining chairs recall American Colonial style.

You also can tour a sturdy stone structure on the next block, where trader Felix Valle lived about the same time, and the 1784 Mason Guibord-Valle House west of the square.

These, and most of Ste. Genevieve's other old homes, survived not out of concern for history, but because they were passed down through families. Many Ste. Genevieve residents trace their ancestry to early settlers, and the whole town celebrates its French heritage with festivals such as Bastille Days in July.

Easy Antiques Hunting

Ste. Genevieve's residents tend to take for granted the 19th-century brick-and-stone buildings in the surrounding business district. Besides housing long-standing local businesses, some of these relative newcomers contain more than two dozen shops and restau-rants that cater to visitors.

At Sara's Antiques, customers can't resist touching tin molded in a ribbons-and-bows pattern that covers the walls, as well as the ceiling overhead. Linens & Lace on the square reminds you of Grandmother's hall closet. Intri-cately embroidered vintage pillow-cases, tablecloths and dresser scarves stack in cupboards and on shelves.

Antique china packs old hutches and decorates mahogany tables at Mr.

Smoked sausage, a specialty of the Oberle family.

FRANK OBERLE

The renovated Southern Hotel, one of the town's historic lodgings.

MIKE PALUCK

Frederic's in a historic home along Market Street. Across the street in another 19th-century home, prints and paintings decorate the walls of Sweet Things, a chocolate shop and showplace for regional artists.

At the Mill Antiques Mart along Main Street, you can browse merchandise from local estate sales and farm auctions. This is the place to find that perfect rolltop desk, old sterling silver flatware or a farmhouse kitchen table.

The menus at Ste. Genevieve's half-dozen restaurants reveal a hearty German flair, unexpected considering the town's French founders. Besides homey fare such as fried chicken and meatloaf, you can sample *knifles* (German liver dumplings) at both the Old Brick House and The Anvil Saloon down the block.

Warm Hospitality

Innkeepers have transformed several of Ste. Genevieve's historic buildings into bed and breakfasts that welcome guests. A red brick Colonial-style mansion built in 1849 has become the Inn St. Gemme Beauvais along Main Street. The Steiger Haus bed and breakfast began its life as the new home of a well-to-do German farmer.

The Southern Hotel at the edge of the square first welcomed travelers in 1805. In those days, the Mississippi River brought paddle wheelers loaded with merchants, traders and other travelers to booming Ste. Genevieve.

Resembling an old plantation house, the hotel took pride in providing hospitality as grand as travelers might find in New Orleans or Natchez, Mississippi. Guests played roulette in the gaming rooms and billiards on the first pool table west of the Mississippi.

Those glory days were long gone by the time St. Louisans Mike and Barbara Hankins bought the vacant hotel in the mid-1980s. The couple restored the inn from top to bottom and opened it to travelers once more. Whimsical folk art and antiques such as a massive carved rosewood headboard and claw-foot bathtubs furnish eight guest rooms. Visitors often pause to admire the gleaming woodwork and stately windows.

Barbara says newcomers continue to be surprised to discover Colonial-era buildings in southeast Missouri. "We're proud of what we've accomplished," Barbara explains. "But we're all just caretakers of these old buildings. We hope we can pass them on to future generations."

By Barbara Morrow.

TRAVEL GUIDE

LOCATION—Southeast Missouri, about 60 miles south of St. Louis' outer suburbs.

LODGINGS—Standard motel rooms around Cape Girardeau, about an hour south along I-55 (Convention & Visitors Bureau, 800/777-0068). Some alternatives: Hotel Ste. Genevieve, clean, bargain-priced rooms in a downtown landmark (doubles from $40, 573/883-3562). Inn St. Gemme Beauvais, seven recently redecorated rooms in a historic mansion (doubles from $89, 800/818-5744). Main Street Inn, renovated 1880s structure with seven guest rooms (doubles from $65, 800/918-9199). The Southern Hotel, eight rooms in a beautifully renovated 1790s hotel (doubles from $80, 800/275-1412).

CAMPING—St. Francois State Park along the Big River near Bonne Terre (about 30 miles west), more than 100 sites, some with hookups; also hiking, horseback riding and canoeing (573/358-2173). Campgrounds at Hawn State Park (20 miles west), a favorite with hikers and wildlife watchers (573/883-3603).

DINING AND FOOD—The Anvil Saloon, a historic building on the square (573/883-7323). Kmetz Home Bakery, German pastries and other treats (closes at noon on weekends, 573/883-3533). Oberle Meats (½ mile west along State-32), special-recipe German sausage, garlic cheese and smoked pork loin (573/883-5656). Show-Me Shop for made-in-Missouri cheeses, wines and other products

(573/883-3096). Old Brick House, a buffet in the oldest brick structure west of the Mississippi River (573/883-2724).

SHOPPING—Linens & Lace, onetime barber shop selling vintage and new trims, collars, table dressings and more (573/883-2675). Mr. Frederic, Ltd., Christmas decorations and collectibles, vintage china and fine antique furniture (573/883-2717). Monia's Unlimited, custom-made quilts and oak furniture on the square (573/883-7874). Sweet Things of Ste. Genevieve, French jams and other imports, as well as fine chocolates and other candies (573/883-7990).

CELEBRATIONS—Bastille Days in July. Christmas Walk in early December.

IN THE AREA—Kaskaskia Island (10 miles south) is the only Illinois soil west of the Mississippi. A shrine houses the 650-pound Liberty Bell of the West, a gift from the king of France in the early 1700s (618/859-3741). Across the river in Illinois, you can visit the Pierre Menard Home State Historic Site, a restored French Colonial mansion that belonged to the state's first lieutenant governor (618/859-3031). Nearby are the remains of Fort Kaskaskia, built during the Revolutionary War (618/859-3741). A ferry crosses the Mississippi from a dock north of town.

INFORMATION—*Great River Road Interpretive Ctr., Tourist Information Office, 66 S. Main St., Ste. Genevieve, MO 63670 (800/373-7007).* ■

MORE GREAT TOWNS

**From frontier settlers to Mark Twain, these towns
showcase Missouri's unique heritage.**

Arrow Rock

Once at the edge of the Missouri River
and an important port on the way west,
Arrow Rock's fortunes declined when
the river shifted course. Now, the entire
town, with just 80 residents, has been
designated a National Historic Landmark. A dozen of the 40 vintage buildings house shops selling collectibles
and works of Missouri crafters.

The Lyceum Theater Company, Missouri's oldest repertory group, per-
forms in a newly expanded playhouse
beside the 1872 Baptist church. The
Old Arrow Rock Tavern, built in 1834,
first served travelers on the Santa Fe
Trail. Today, diners drive for miles for
homey specialties there such as country ham, fried chicken and catfish.

Innkeepers have transformed three
historic houses into bed and breakfasts.
At the Downover Bed and Breakfast
Inn, you can stay in homey rooms or a
cottage with a kitchen.

*Location—Central Missouri, about
40 miles northwest of Columbia.*

*Information—Friends of Arrow
Rock, Box 124, Arrow Rock, MO 65320
(660/837-3231).*

Carthage

After the Civil War, Carthage (population: 10,750) boomed on lead and zinc
mining. Reputedly, the town boasted
more millionaires per capita than anywhere else in the nation. Along Grand
Avenue, you pass gracious homes built
during that time. The Leggett House, a
restored 1901 stone mansion, now
hosts visitors as a bed and breakfast.

A fortresslike courthouse towers
over the town square. Try Carthage
Deli & Ice Cream in an 1868 bank
building for tasty Reuben sandwiches
and old-fashioned malts. Tea and
Truffles, an intimate tearoom, serves
sandwiches and pastries.

Southwest of town, you can visit the
Precious Moments Chapel, with elaborate murals and stained-glass windows
by Sam Butcher, creator of the popular
wide-eyed figurines.

*Location—Southwest Missouri, 2
miles east of Joplin.*

**Tom, Huck and
Becky wannabes
compete at Tom
Sawyer Days in
Hannibal.**

CHET HANCHETT

Information—Carthage Chamber of Commerce, 107 E. Third St., Carthage, MO 64836 (417/358-2373).

Hannibal

Samuel Clemens hadn't acquired the pen name Mark Twain when he left the northeast Missouri town of Hannibal. But he never forgot this Mississippi River town of 18,000, which carefully preserves his memory.

The 11-block historic district in the center of Hannibal reminds you of small towns during Twain's time. You can admire the white picket fence Tom Sawyer made famous and visit Twain's boyhood home. Shops selling crafts and gifts occupy old-time storefronts.

Down at the cobblestone landing, the replica paddle wheeler *Mark Twain* plies the river on sightseeing tours.

Eateries here specialize in hearty cooking. The Ole Planters Restaurant serves plate lunches, ribs and other barbecue on weekends and 10 kinds of hamburgers. You can stay at opulent Garth Woodside Mansion, one of five bed and breakfasts.

Location—Northeast Missouri, about 100 miles north of St. Louis.

Information—Hannibal Visitors & Convention Bureau, 505 N. Third St., Hannibal, MO 63401 (314/221-2477).

Hermann

More than a century ago, immigrants from Germany chose this site because it reminded them of the Rhine River Valley. Now, this town of 2,800, with its sturdy brick buildings and graceful church spires, is home to four wineries. Dine at Stone Hill Winery's Vintage 1847 restaurant in the original carriage house on a hill overlooking town.

Galleries and shops fill the historic downtown with everything from antiques to handwoven rugs and German imports. Travelers choose from more than 3 dozen bed and breakfasts in town and nearby, including Market Street Bed and Breakfast.

Location—East-central Missouri, about 60 miles west of St. Louis.

Information—Hermann Tourism Group, Visitor Information Center, 306 Market St., Hermann, MO 65041 (800/932-8687).

Kimmswick

In the late 1800s, residents of this tiny Mississippi River town lamented when railroads and highways bypassed their village. Now, Kimmswick, with just 196 residents, proudly calls itself the "Town That Time Forgot."

Just steps from the mighty river, this village sprouted hotels and saloons to entertain St. Louisans, who arrived by riverboat in the mid-1800s. Today, Victorian homes and renovated storefronts contain more than two dozen shops. Two Sundays a month, you can visit historic homes on walking tours.

The Blue Owl Restaurant and Bakery serves legendary homemade soups and desserts. The Old House Restaurant, a 200-year-old log structure, is known for juicy prime rib and special-recipe fried chicken.

Location—Eastern Missouri, 30 miles south of St. Louis.

Information—Kimmswick Merchants Assoc., Box 116, Kimmswick, MO 63053 (314/464-6464). Most stores and restaurants close Mondays.

St. Charles

Although hemmed in by interstates and surrounded by suburban sprawl, the heart of this Missouri River community of 54,000—Old Main Street and the adjacent Frenchtown Historic District—retains a small-town charm and appears much as it might have a century ago.

Along Main Street paralleling the river, 10 blocks of vintage buildings showcase dozens of specialty, craft and collectibles shops, bakeries and candy stores. Restaurants such as the antique-filled Mother-in-Law House in an 1866 brick cottage specialize in gracious hospitality. The adjacent Frenchtown area is an enclave of antiques shops.

You can stay at two Main Street bed and breakfasts: Boone's Lick Trail Inn, an 1840 landmark home, and St. Charles House, an elegant inn in the heart of the business district.

Location—Eastern Missouri, about 20 miles northwest of St. Louis.

Information—Greater St. Charles Convention & Visitors Bureau, 230 S. Main St., Saint Charles, MO 63301 (800/366-2427). ∎

NEBRASKA

ASHLAND • MINDEN
NEBRASKA CITY • WILBER

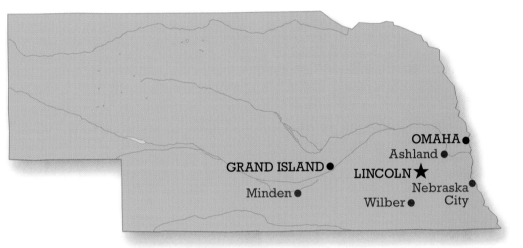

It's easy to think of Nebraska as two states in one: the larger-than-life landscapes and wide-open spaces of the high plains that once challenged early settlers moving west, and the gentler countryside of rolling hills and river valleys to the east.

It's in eastern Nebraska that you'll not only discover the Cornhusker State's two major cities (Omaha and Lincoln), but also tidy farms and the postcard-pretty small towns featured here. Settled amid peaceful river valleys, each of these communities takes almost as much pride in preserving its heritage as it does in sharing that past—and more modern attractions—with visitors.

For information about additional Nebraska towns that you can visit, contact: *Nebraska Travel & Tourism, Dept. of Economic Development, 700 S. 16th St., Box 94666, Lincoln, NE 68509 (800/228-4307)*.

NEBRASKA CITY

A rich pioneer past and the legacy of an early conservationist make this town a treat to visit.

On a lazy summer afternoon, Nebraska City drowses under a canopy of green. Ash, cottonwood and oak trees shade the neat rows of turn-of-the-century buildings downtown, along with the surrounding neighborhoods of gaily painted Victorian homes.

J. Sterling Morton, a frontier journalist who established Arbor Day, founded a homestead here in 1855. He helped nurture this Missouri River town's devotion to trees and green spaces. Morton's mansion, which now is a state park, crowns one of the town's many hills.

This community of 6,500 prospered on river traffic and the nation's expansion west, weathering the rowdy frontier era and the explosive days before the Civil War. You can walk streets that curve and dip over and around the town's hills to buildings that are legacies of those early times. The street system can be confusing, but that's part of Nebraska City's appeal. Twisting lanes paved in brick seem to invite you to linger and browse.

Historic Downtown

Pieces of history lace the town, especially along Central Avenue (Old Main Street), where storefronts create a patchwork of colors and textures. A red brick facade with arched windows neighbors a limestone structure decorated with elaborate cornices.

The Farmers Bank, resembling a small castle with its turrets and bay windows, once was Nebraska City's post office. With its distinctive white cupola, the Otoe County Courthouse, the oldest public building in the state, towers over a manicured square just down the street.

Shopping at factory outlets draws visitors here, and you'll discover five outlet centers downtown. Bargain hunters snap up merchandise that ranges from fancy wedding gowns to work socks.

Boutiques and stores showcasing locally made crafts also take their places in the historic district. Eight antiques dealers sell a variety of merchandise, as diverse as dainty linens and rustic primitives.

One block south of Central Avenue, woolens pack two levels at the Pendleton Outlet. Next door, you can sample from-scratch muffins and sip espresso and other special brews at the Coffee Press. Old typewriters and cameras on display recall the 1920s building's days as a newspaper office. Upstairs, browse specialty shops.

For more bargain shopping, travel south of town to the $5-million outlet mall, which includes 10 stores.

Trolley Tours
Link Attractions

Buses that resemble old-fashioned trolleys shuttle passengers to historic sites and shopping areas around town. Along the way, drivers regale visitors with stories about Nebraska City's rich history and attractions.

The town's unusual layout, one driver explains, results partly from the geography of its riverside location, as well as the fact that Nebraska City was three separate towns until 1857.

Long before that, the region's gentle hills and wooded bluffs provided excellent hunting for Plains Indians and later for European fur trappers. Lewis and Clark came up the Missouri in 1803. Soon, prairie schooners and steamboats brimming with eager settlers lined the riverbanks.

Nebraska City flourished as a trading post and riverboat stop. Two of the most important pioneer trails began here and connected with the famous Oregon Trail.

In a single day, more than 800 ox-drawn wagons departed for trails west. Steamboats pulled into the town's docks with cargoes to be loaded on overland freighters. Russell, Majors and Waddell Freighting Co., creator of the Pony Express and one of the major forces in settling the West, owned many of the wagons.

Visitors take horse-drawn carriage tours of the grounds at Arbor Lodge.

Today, in that company's 1859 head-quarters building, the Old Freighter's Museum documents Nebraska City's history as a transportation hub. You'll see ox yokes, old maps and a copy of the Pony Express oath.

The Underground Railroad also made its mark here. The Nebraska City cabin of Allen Mayhew, constructed in the 1850s of stout cottonwood logs, sheltered many runaway slaves. The cabin still stands and is now on the grounds of John Brown's Cave and Historical Village.

You can descend into a winding reconstructed tunnel, where slaves hid before escaping in the night via nearby Table Creek. On a 7-acre village green along the creek, you'll discover a farm-house, livery, blacksmith shop, church and train depot of a 1900s rural community. Old-time shops make up the Evening on Main Street exhibit.

Grand Homes

In its 1800s heyday, Nebraska City teemed with pioneers, bushwhackers, goldrushers and gunslingers. They packed the town's newly built sa-loons, stores and boardinghouses. Merchants, bankers, attorneys and freight haulers prospered. Their wealth endures in the more than 300 homes and buildings listed in the National Register of Historic Places. You'll see a variety of architectural styles, including Queen Anne, Gothic Revival and Italianate.

You can tour the modest Taylor-Wessel-Bickel House, one of several open to visitors. The tidy red brick home, among the town's oldest, survives as a fine example of Greek Revival architecture. Its pine-board floors, hand-hewn staircases and richly carved walnut furniture reflect the skill of woodworkers long ago.

An expansive park surrounds Wild-wood House, a restored Victorian country gentleman's home that banker Jasper Ware built in 1869. Two parlors graced with Oriental rugs, lace and velvet recall the dignified, unhurried Victorian era. The whitewashed barn, once used as a dairy, now is an art gallery and gift shop, featuring crafts and regional artists' works.

In this historic river town, even a

Buy a bag of fall's favorite fruit at the J. Sterling Morton Orchard.

BOB BARRETT

Nebraska City's War Memorial Building.

ROBERT HUGHES

visit to the cemetery yields intriguing discoveries. Wyuka Cemetery includes one of the most unusual collections of monuments in the nation. The most prominent is a 20-foot stone tree, a memorial to J. Sterling Morton, who died in 1902. There's also a full-size granite rolltop desk, which marks the grave of N.S. Harding, writer of the state's first insurance policy.

Morton's Palace

Arbor Lodge, Morton's 52-room manor, stands amid tree-studded lawns and formal gardens. Now a state historical park, the neo-Colonial mansion began as a four-room frame house. In 1903, Joy Morton, the oldest Morton son and the founder of the Morton Salt Company, completed the three-story building that visitors see today. The white stucco palace, with its three wings and hand-carved woodwork, showcases Parisian tapestries, Tiffany glassware, glistening silver, china collections and original paintings.

The 65-acre grounds overlook the Missouri River and the Iowa bluffs. A trail meanders through an arboretum with 260 identified varieties of trees, some that Morton himself planted.

Enjoy the cool tranquillity of the 1-acre Pine Grove or smell the roses as you walk along gently curving brick paths in the Italian Terraced Garden. You can visit the Carriage House to view a traditional surrey, an Overland stagecoach and a carriage that President Grover Cleveland used. Throughout the estate, you'll discover peaceful spots to relax and picnic.

The Arbor Day Legacy

Another Morton legacy, the National Arbor Day Foundation, recently opened the $15-million Lied Conference Center. This full-service resort, which welcomes the public for overnight stays, has been the site of international meetings about the environment. The architecture recalls classic national park lodges, but with its own unique Frank Lloyd Wright flavor.

Douglas fir columns, trusses and beams frame the grand lobby, and a massive limestone fireplace soars 35 feet to the ceiling. Quotations by historic figures about the importance of trees rim the upper walls.

Exposed timber runs throughout the building, which is furnished with stately Mission-style pieces. Each area highlights a type of wood such as warm butternut in the dining room and rich black walnut in the lounge. A veranda provides a sweeping view of Table Creek Forest and Arbor Lodge.

Arbor Day Farm, including the J. Sterling Morton Orchard, surrounds the conference center. You can follow a tree-identification trail, step inside historic barns or browse in the Apple House gift shop. The Apple House Pie Garden sells homemade pies and cider slushes. In fall, you can watch apple-sorting and cider-making.

The Morton Orchard is one of three local commercial apple orchards. During the harvest, roadside produce stands overflowing with apples, cherries and cider jugs dot the surrounding country lanes.

Ask about a scenic 40-mile driving tour along twisting backroads that fan out from Nebraska City. In the fall, this route takes you through the woods glowing with autumn reds and ambers and fields gone golden. But the drive is just as enjoyable any time of year.

By Michelle Carr.

TRAVEL GUIDE

LOCATION—Southeast Nebraska, 42 miles south of Omaha.

LODGINGS—Whispering Pines Bed and Breakfast, 100-year-old home with five guest rooms on 6-acre grounds that include four ponds and fountains (doubles from $50, 402/873-5850). Lied Conference Center, striking lodge with a dining room, 96 rooms and suites, and paths linking carefully tended grounds with adjoining Arbor Day Farm (doubles from $99, 800/546-5433). Apple Inn near downtown, 65 spacious rooms (doubles from $45, 800/659-4446). Days Inn, 29-room chain motel (doubles from $46, 402/873-6656).

CAMPING—Riverview Marina, a serene, tree-covered campground at the Missouri River's edge (402/873-7222). Indian Cave State Park (40 miles south of Nebraska City), 3,000 acres named for a sandstone overhang marked with Native American rock carvings (402/883-2575).

DINING AND FOOD—Ulbrick's Cafe, legendary panfried chicken and creamed vegetables served family-style (402/873-5458). Embers Steakhouse and Lounge, tender prime rib and juicy steaks (402/873-6416). Lied Conference Center dining room, steaks, seafood and a lavish Sunday brunch (402/873-8740). Teresa's Family Restaurant, home-style pies (402/873-9100).

SHOPPING—VF Factory Outlet, State-2 and US-75 South (402/873-7727). Apple Core, five rooms of fine-art prints, collectibles, soaps and candies (402/873-7600).

IN THE AREA—*The Spirit of Brownville* riverboat cruises the lazy Missouri from the historic village of Brownville (20 miles south of Nebraska City). Choose from an afternoon sightseeing jaunt, the captain's dinner cruise or a moonlight dinner excursion with entertainment (402/825-6441).

CELEBRATIONS—Apple Jack Festival, harvest celebration with a parade, crafts and antiques shows and an apple-pie-making contest in September. Arbor Day Celebration, a fair and festival with an environmental theme, in April.

INFORMATION—*Nebraska City Convention & Visitors Bureau, 806 First Ave., Nebraska City, NE 68410 (800/514-9113).* ■

MORE GREAT TOWNS

This trio of towns recalls Nebraska's proud past and salutes its rich ethnic heritage.

Ashland

Woods that climb to sandstone-and-clay bluffs cradle this lazy river town of 2,100 near the junction of the Platte River and Salt Creek. Prospectors on the Oxbow Trail crossed Salt Creek on their way to the Oregon Trail and the California gold fields in the 1800s.

The town's red brick Silver Street took its name from the "Silver Gang," who opened businesses here in 1855 after working in Colorado's silver mines. Today, along Ashland's three-block-long business district, lantern-style streetlights flank brick buildings that remain from the early days.

Craft and country-art stores welcome shoppers. You'll find handmade quilts and needlepoint gifts in one and wildlife paintings and drawings of historic buildings in another. Just north of downtown, drive shady Clay and Adams streets to view stately homes.

Granny's Cafe serves steak-and-eggs breakfasts. The Gateway Inn is known for fried chicken. You can stay at Bundy's Bed and Breakfast or at Nebraska's newest state park, Eugene T. Mahoney, 3 miles southeast. The park surrounds a three-story lodge that commands wooded bluffs above the river.

Location—Southeast Nebraska, 30 miles southwest of Omaha.

Information—Ashland Chamber of Commerce, 1409 Silver St., Ashland, NE 68003 (402/944-2050).

Minden

Trees line the square that's the site of the white-domed Kearney County Courthouse in this south-central Nebraska town of 2,800. Along nearby

Reminders of pioneer days at Fort Kearney State Historical Park, north of Minden.

MIKE WHYE

streets, homes that doctors and lawyers built in the late 1800s still gleam like gems from yesterday.

Most visitors stop by Harold Warp Pioneer Village. Billed on highway signs as "Nebraska's No. 1 attraction," the village calls itself the nation's only museum of progress. More than 50,000 items in 28 buildings catalog the development of technology, from electric lights to sewing machines, old-time tractors and the oldest steam-powered merry-go-round in the nation.

For a hefty cut of Nebraska beef, try Shay's. J.J.'s City Cafe has earned a reputation for hearty breakfasts.

Location—South-central Nebraska, 21 miles southeast of Kearney.

Information—Minden Chamber of Commerce, Box 375, Minden, NE 68959 (308/832-1811).

Wilber

Recorded polka music serenades downtown shoppers, and Czech names and designs decorate storefronts in this southeast Nebraska town of 1,500 known as the "Czech Capital of the United States." But the prosperous businesses, tidy homes and stores, and clean-swept sidewalks recall small-town America of the 1950s.

Just off Main Street, the Czech Museum showcases heirlooms from the town's founders. Mannequins wear intricately embroidered antique costumes brought from the old country. Historic furnishings fill room settings, and you can view a Czech doll collection. Nearby shops stock Czech imports, from jewelry set with Czech garnets to dolls in authentic costumes.

A block north stands the Hotel Wilber, an 1895 brick building with a wide veranda. Original polished woodwork frames 10 guest rooms that feature turn-of-the-century furnishings. *Kolaches* (fruit-filled Czech pastries) star at the inn's enormous breakfasts.

Location—Southeast Nebraska, about 40 miles southwest of Lincoln.

Information—Wilber Chamber of Commerce, Box 1164, Wilber, NE 68465 (888/4-WILBER). ■

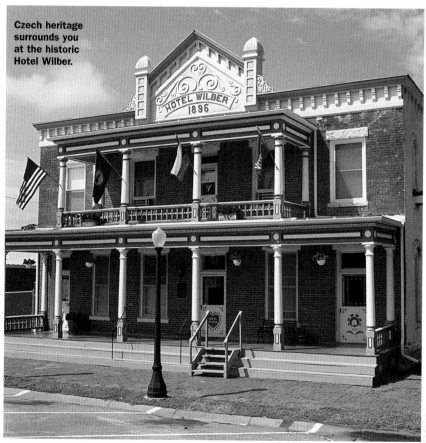

Czech heritage surrounds you at the historic Hotel Wilber.

MIKE WHYE

OHIO

BERLIN • BURTON • COSHOCTON
GRAND RAPIDS • GRANVILLE • LEBANON
MARIETTA • MEDINA • OBERLIN
PUT-IN-BAY • YELLOW SPRINGS

With Cleveland, Cincinnati, Columbus, Toledo, Dayton and Akron, Ohio claims more major cities than any other Midwest state. But those metropolises don't overshadow appealing small towns across the Buckeye State. Settlers from the East founded communities resembling New England villages. Other towns sprang up at strategic locations along rivers and canals, from the shores of Lake Erie in the north to the misty hills and hollows along the Ohio River to the south.

For information about additional Ohio small towns you can visit, contact: *Ohio Div. of Travel & Tourism, Box 1001, Columbus, OH 43216-1001 (800/BUCKEYE).*

GRANVILLE

Like a scene straight from New England, this town rises amid the hills of central Ohio.

When New England's population tripled after the Revolutionary War, easterners from Granville, Massachusetts, and nearby Granby, Connecticut, commissioned a party to scout the western reaches of the new nation. Those pioneers unloaded their oxcarts amid central Ohio's gently rolling hills in November 1805.

Deacon Timothy Rose and his followers set about raising another Granville in this wilderness. The pioneers harnessed Raccoon Creek to power sawmills, dug clay for bricks and quarried gray limestone from Sugar Loaf Hill for buildings that still stand. They platted the village around a town square like the ones they'd known back East and reverently built a church on each corner.

Today, these early pioneers' vision and industry remain as the foundation of the town of Granville (population: 4,353). It's a bit of New England located east of Columbus amid central Ohio's Welsh Hills.

Around Downtown

The business district, which unfolds along Broadway, the main east-west thoroughfare, seems made for strolling. A rainbow of awnings decorates turn-of-the-century facades, stately with tall windows and elaborate cornices. In summer, pots overflowing with geraniums dot the broad walkway. Window displays entice passersby into galleries, antiques shops and restaurants. You'll discover more than 2 dozen specialty stores along Broadway and intersecting streets.

One of the town's early schools evolved into Denison University. The college's majestic Greek Revival buildings crown a hill that rises above the center of town. Shady walks take you to the campus chapel and 11 other buildings that are listed in the National Register of Historic Places.

Along Broadway, shoppers step across tread-worn sandstone thresholds to browse and buy folk-art furnishings

at Hare Hollow or to enjoy a rich ice cream cone at Victoria's Olde Tyme Deli and Cafe. Marble tables and wire-back chairs distinguish this old-fashioned ice cream parlor.

Visitors who long to take home a bit of the town's heritage scout A Place in History on North Prospect for vintage books and prints. Sensibilities in the onetime Village Hall on South Main Street stocks linens, furnishings and gifts.

Greystone Country House, also along Main, features antiques, primitive furnishings and folk art, including whimsical carved Santas. At Cherry Traditions along Cherry Street, accessories you can buy—from brass trivets to hand-turned four-poster beds of gleaming dark wood—recall the refined look of furnishings and housewares from Colonial Williamsburg.

Landmark Lodgings

The Granville Inn and The Buxton Inn, historic lodgings and restaurants from different eras, face each other across Broadway. The 1812 Buxton Inn, painted a traffic-stopping yet historically authentic hot coral, was the first post office and a thriving stagecoach stop in Granville's early days.

Recognized as Ohio's oldest inn continuously operating in its original structure, The Buxton Inn has grown to include five historic buildings surrounding a central courtyard. The complex is a fantasy of cascading blossoms and bubbling fountains.

Owners Orville and Audrey Orr have restored details such as the original reception desk. Antiques furnish the 25 guest rooms. The dining room serves hearty breakfasts and dinners that have a decidedly French flair.

Across the street, the Tudor-style Granville Inn appears older than The Buxton Inn, but actually it's a 1924 recreation of a 16th-century English manor house. Coal tycoon John Sutphin Jones built the inn to accommodate the overflow from his estate down

Swasey
Observatory
at Denison
University, which
crowns a hill
above town.

the road. Jones held legendary gatherings at which guests such as pianist Sergei Rachmaninov performed.

Dining at The Granville Inn, you feel as if you're a guest at one of those lavish affairs. Finely carved oak paneling adorns the dining room. Dishes such as the rich chicken Oscar arrive on regal-looking stoneware.

Museum Browsing

Fittingly housed in the town's oldest building, the 1816 Alexandria Bank, The Granville Historical Society Museum documents the story of Granville and its most prominent "citizen," Denison University.

In 1831, Baptists created the Granville Literary and Theological Institution. That school became Denison University, a renowned liberal-arts college with an enrollment of 1,800.

The museum also houses the town's oldest artifact, a simple table hewn by one of Granville's first settlers. The black walnut slab stands on legs as knobby as a newborn colt's.

The Granville Life-Style Museum occupies an 1870 home that belonged to the Root-Devenney-Robinson family. Members of the family traced their lineage back to Martin Root, the driver of one of the wagons that came to Granville from Massachusetts in 1805.

The museum displays quilts, clothes and furniture collected from the time the family arrived in Ohio until the last member died in 1981. So large was the cache that it took curators 13 years to work their way through the last trunk.

Historic Architecture

The National Register of Historic Places lists 120 of Granville's build-

Owners Audrey and Orville Orr welcome you at The Buxton Inn.

AL TEUFEN

ings. The Licking County Historical Society is restoring one of the area's greatest architectural treasures, the 1842 Robbins Hunter Museum. This 27-room mansion is a replica of a Greek temple. As the work is completed, the society will open rooms to the public one by one.

Volunteer guides at the museum proudly point out a 200-year-old London tall-case clock of gleaming tiger maple, as well as the home's original 1845 mahogany rope bed. Ohio Governor and future President William McKinley once slept in it.

A walking tour along Broadway and the surrounding streets takes you to 35 homes and other buildings. Some of these vintage structures number among the oldest in Granville.

In 1824, the Mower House, a Federal-style mansion, cost $650—a princely sum then—to build. Residents call a trio of late-1800s beauties along Prospect Street "the three sisters," because they share the same fanciful Victorian style.

Homeowners groom these gems with seemingly endless renovations, painstakingly duplicating historically accurate color schemes and authentic trims. Flowers that line the immaculate streets and gardens that bloom amid manicured lawns complete the peaceful setting.

For a moment, you feel as if you're not just looking at a scene from history, but that you and Granville truly are part of the past.

By Betsa Marsh.

BERLIN

Leave city life behind when you visit this Amish town, surrounded by peaceful countryside.

Just an hour's drive south of Cleveland's suburbs, the highways narrow and strike off through green fields. Along the roadways, yellow diamonds with black horse-and-buggy silhouettes begin to appear, looking more like promises than warnings. It's time to slow down. You're in Holmes County, the heart of north-central Ohio's Amish country.

Millersburg, with its imposing courthouse, is the county seat. But Berlin, with 3,000 residents (just 7 miles east), is the hub of the largest Amish community in the world.

Just as their ancestors did, the 15,000 Amish who live on surrounding farms and in even smaller towns reject worldly trappings. They believe that cars, electricity and other modern conveniences might undermine the simplicity and pacifism that form the cornerstones of their faith. That means Amish life hasn't changed much for a century.

In Berlin, you can sample hearty Amish-style cooking and browse a variety of shops packed with Amish crafts and handiwork. Surrounding Holmes County hamlets, where buggies still outnumber the cars, return visitors to a slower, simpler time.

Bustling with Business

Berlin's business district, a mix of new stores, restaurants and vintage homes converted into shops, stretches along State-39, following the crest of a ridge. Hundreds of quilts spin on racks and stack neatly on shelves at Helping Hands Quilt Shop and Museum. Traditional Amish patterns—geometric shapes in bold reds, blacks and other deep, rich colors—mix with familiar designs such as the "log cabin" and "wedding ring."

If you don't see exactly what you're looking for, the area's Amish seamstresses gladly will make quilts to order. Money from these sales goes to Amish and Mennonite charities

(the two sects share common roots and continue to maintain close ties).

A half-dozen furniture shops scatter amid the other stores, showcasing sturdy handcrafted pieces of oak and pine. You'll see cupboards, rolltop desks and kitchen tables that are stout enough for the most lively family.

"We don't want to build things just to be used for a few years and worn out," one woodworker explains. "We hope these will be heirlooms."

Bakeries stock breads, flaky pastries and Amish favorites such as peanut butter pie. Cheese shops sell buttery Swiss that's made with milk from Amish dairy farms.

At mealtime, visitors can join local residents at the Dutch Harvest Restaurant. Waitresses wearing the Mennonite women's traditional starched caps serve plentiful portions of baked ham, roast beef swimming in gravy and freshly whipped mashed potatoes.

Amish Ways

Visitors' cars creep behind square black buggies making their way through town. Amish men wear beards, broad-brimmed black hats and homemade trousers. Women cover their heads with bonnets and dress in unadorned, calf-length cotton frocks—darker colors for older women and lighter shades for girls.

Plain dress, horse-and-buggy travel and other customs that set the Amish apart stem from their deep religious beliefs. *Behalt*, the information center east of Berlin along County-77, helps explain the events that shaped the Amish and Mennonite ways of life. A sweeping mural that rings the center's dome depicts members of both faiths fleeing religious persecution in Europe and the hardships of the journey to the New World.

Most of the Amish are shy about responding to visitors' questions concerning their ways, and their religion discourages unnecessary contact with

Black Amish buggies routinely roll through town.

outsiders. That's one of the reasons Jo Ann Hershberger and her family established Schrock's Amish Farm and Home on the east edge of Berlin.

"We're proud of our heritage, and this is a chance to share it with others," says Jo Ann, who's the granddaughter of an Amish bishop.

As you walk through the complex's authentically furnished farmhouse, a guide explains the differences between branches of the Amish and Mennonite faiths and the reasoning behind some of the Amish customs. Visitors pile into an Amish buggy for rides around the farm. The horse plods along the dirt path, despite a youngster's pleas to pick up the pace.

"What do you want to go so fast for?" the genuinely puzzled Amish driver asks good-naturedly.

Backroads Discoveries

Just beyond the bustle of Berlin's main street, Holmes County's quiet rural character endures. Two-lane roads meander past teams of Belgian draft horses that farmers drive to work their fields. White farmhouses sprout additions to shelter several generations of the same Amish families.

Windmills spin overhead, pumping water to busy Amish kitchens. Hand-lettered signs point to small businesses: a blacksmith shop, wheelwright and steam-powered lumber mill. They thrive far from the rush of conventional traffic. A one-room schoolhouse stands half-painted along one backroad. Amish children attend classes there.

You can follow these twisting two-lanes to other towns and farms where the Amish continue to live as they have for generations.

On most days along the route to Mount Hope (7 miles northeast of Berlin along County-77), you'll poke along at a steady pace behind Amish buggies. But on Wednesdays, auction

Your hosts at the Charm Countryview Inn: Paul and Naomi Miller, and their son, Matthew.

DOYLE YODER

day in this town of 230, brace yourself for a traffic jam. Cars line up behind horse-drawn wagons swaying under loads of hay and buggies packed with pies and loaves of bread for sale.

Find a seat in the cavernous auction house and watch as loads of eggs or pairs of calves go to the highest bidders. A flea market occupies the surrounding grounds. Stalls sell merchandise such as baked goods, produce from Amish gardens and carefully knitted shawls and children's caps.

Old World Charm

The village of Charm slumbers in a valley just south of Berlin. But 30 years ago, Amanda Miller awoke the community with a start when she began selling her quilts to the "English," as Amish call outsiders.

A screen door slaps behind you as you enter Amanda's white cottage shop along Charm's main street. Bins and racks hold quilting supplies. Beautiful quilts hang from the walls and ceiling.

Times have changed, Amanda acknowledges. "It used to be, you couldn't give away a length of red broadcloth in these parts," she says. Now, bright bolts of calico and paisley form a rainbow against the rear wall.

From a distance, you might mistake the Charm Countryview Inn, located just southeast of Charm, for any of the area's Amish farms. Paul and Naomi Miller, Mennonites whose ancestors helped settle Holmes County, welcome visitors to the 15-room inn.

With a slight accent that hints at the German that was his first language growing up in an Amish home, Paul says earnestly that he and Naomi wanted to share something of their way of life with visitors.

"We want this to be a place where you slow down and come away refreshed," Paul tells a guest.

That's the best part about visiting the town of Berlin and the Amish country that surrounds it.

By Barbara Morrow.

TRAVEL GUIDE

LOCATION—North-central Ohio, about 90 miles south of Cleveland.

LODGINGS—Standard motels available. Some alternatives: Amish Country Inn, 50 rooms with locally made furnishings (doubles from $70, 330/893-3000). Guggisberg Swiss Inn, a recently opened motel near Charm (doubles from $79, 330/893-3600). The Inn at Honey Run, a pampering contemporary inn and restaurant *(see Dining and Food)* near Millersburg (doubles from $95, 800/468-6639). Carlisle Village Inn, individually decorated Victorian-style rooms in nearby Walnut Creek (doubles from $330, 216/893-3636). Charm Countryview Inn, a 15-room bed and breakfast just south of Berlin near Charm (doubles from $75, 216/330-3003).

CAMPING—Scenic Hills RV Park (1 mile east of Berlin), more than 40 sites with hookups (330/893-3258).

DINING AND FOOD—Der Bake Oven, freshly baked pies and breads in Berlin (330/893-3365). Der Dutchman, for hearty Amish-style fare in nearby Walnut Creek (330/893-2981). Dutch Harvest Restaurant, serving home-style meals, along with their renowned apple pie at a casual family restaurant in Berlin (330/893-3333). Guggisberg Cheese in Berlin, acclaimed baby Swiss (330/893-2500). The Inn at Honey Run near Millersburg, lighter fare elegantly prepared (800/468-6639).

CELEBRATIONS—Christmas in Berlin, Friday and Saturday after Thanksgiving and December Saturdays before Christmas.

INFORMATION—*Amish Country Visitors Bureau, Box 177, Berlin, OH 44610 (330/893-3467). Holmes County Chamber of Commerce, 5798 County-77, Millersburg, OH 44654 (330/674-3975).* ■

LEBANON

A thriving southwest Ohio community with a cherished past that's preserved throughout town.

The U.S. was just toddling toward its 25th anniversary and most of the Midwest remained a wilderness when Lebanon first welcomed travelers as a stop along southwest Ohio's old stagecoach road.

The Golden Lamb, a log structure that became the budding town's second tavern, opened its doors in 1803. By 1815, a brick building replaced the log tavern, and the new hotel had gained a nationwide reputation for fine hospitality. Storefronts and businesses in Federal and Greek Revival styles rose along wide boulevards. Prosperous residents built lavish homes in nearby neighborhoods.

Today, Lebanon thrives as an energetic community of 10,000. But the town center and historic neighborhoods have retained their graciousness from the 19th century.

The red brick Golden Lamb, with white pillars in front, still presides over downtown, which claims some of the Midwest's oldest buildings. Storefronts, homes and churches recall the years from the early 1800s through the turn of the century, with a scattering of more recent additions mixed in. Shops sell antiques, artwork and collectibles almost as interesting and varied as the buildings that line Lebanon's streets.

Stagecoach-Stop Beginnings

Lebanon's forward-thinking planners platted a wide swath for Broadway, so stagecoach drivers easily could turn their rigs in front of The Golden Lamb. The street still is four lanes wide, with room for parking on both sides.

Since those early days, the hotel has served as a cornerstone for downtown, attracting travelers and businesses. More than a century later, the imposing inn remains a treasured landmark.

The Golden Lamb rises over the intersection of Broadway and Main streets, Lebanon's major thoroughfares. Next door, flower-lined brick walkways meander through Lebanon City Park. It was dedicated in 1802. The town hall and the imposing city library command other corners of the busy intersection.

A turn-of-the-century train station anchors the south end of Broadway. From the station, you can take a ride aboard the Turtle Creek Valley Railway. Restored red cars from the 1930s make 1-hour trips through the surrounding wooded hills and meadows dancing with wildflowers.

Golden Hospitality

In the early 1800s, stagecoach passengers instructed drivers leaving Cincinnati and Columbus to simply "Drive to the Sign of The Golden Lamb." The way station gained a reputation for warm hospitality, accommodations that were grand for the day and tasty, plentiful fare. Ten presidents, authors that included Mark Twain and Charles Dickens, plus luminaries such as politician Henry Clay, stayed in the elegant rooms.

Today, The Golden Lamb welcomes visitors in that same gracious style. Most of the18 rooms are named for the hotel's famous guests. Amid Victorian decor in the Dickens Room, a massive canopy bed reaches almost to the 12-foot-high ceiling. A simple four-poster is the centerpiece of the DeWitt Clinton Room, named for a former governor of New York state.

Downstairs, four dining rooms, each decorated with a different theme, serve classics such as roast turkey, skillet-fried chicken and prime rib. Freshly baked rolls accompany each meal.

Pegs holding all sorts of antique kitchen gadgets decorate the walls of the Shaker Room. It's dedicated to a community of Shakers that once flourished in nearby Union Village. In the Dickens Dining Room, scenes from the author's novels adorn the walls. Food arrives on china that's decorated with ornate Victorian-era patterns.

On the fourth floor, you can view Shaker furnishings that the inn's for-

Gaslights line Lebanon's streets, which showcase some of the Midwest's oldest buildings.

mer owner collected. After dinner, you're welcome to climb the steps and have a look. Doors are purposely left open to unoccupied rooms so visitors can peek inside.

Shopping Treasures

Along surrounding streets, you may discover early 1800s pieces and other rarities in more than 50 antiques and specialty stores. Shops sell popular collectibles, but visitors also find artworks and one-of-a-kind items.

The Turtle Creek Gallery, located a block north of the hotel along Broadway, showcases local artists' paintings, plus sculptures and baskets crafters from across the nation created.

Sign of Our Times, another shop along Broadway, almost always starts browsers reminiscing. The shop's 20th-century collectibles include toys

from the 1940s and '50s, as well as TV and movie memorabilia. Down the street, Type-tiques, Inc., stocks old printer's type and symbols, ranging from lead-block letters once used to spell out newspaper headlines to engravings of maps and cartoons.

In the Golden Turtle Chocolate Factory, a glass case that runs the length of the store displays tray after tray of enticing chocolate shapes: tennis rackets, cartoon characters, alligators and even a dinosaur.

A candy-cane-striped awning greets diners at the Village Ice Cream Parlor, an old-time soda fountain across from The Golden Lamb. As you wait for a frosty malt, study the grainy photographs on the wall. The pictures show Lebanon around the turn of the century. In many ways, the town hasn't changed much since then.

Ted and Joy Kossouji at their Golden Turtle Chocolate Factory.

TONY WALSH

Small-Town Character

So much of the past survives because residents cherish their heritage. When other towns tore down old buildings and courted industry in recent decades, Lebanon resisted development that might have damaged its image.

In a Federal-style building along Broadway, the Warren County Historical Society Museum is a well-organized community attic. The first floor re-creates a 19th-century Ohio town. Browse the watchmaker's display of vintage timepieces or visit a tinsmith's workshop, where you might have purchased a cramped-looking bathtub like the one on exhibit.

Upstairs, the Shaker Gallery showcases furniture and handiwork. Graceful handcrafted pieces are arranged as they might have been in a Shaker home. Another area of the museum showcases Shaker innovations such as a better rat trap and an ingenious broom press.

In the nearby East End Historic District, 19th-century homes in taffy-candy colors resemble pampered princesses, surrounded by manicured lawns. With turrets, towers and fancy trim, Gothics and Queen Annes upstage sensible Greek Revival sisters.

A walking tour takes you past many of these beauties, as well as stately 19th-century churches and some of Lebanon's oldest structures. You'll see the 1807 John Tharpe House and a classic Revival home built around a log cabin.

Lebanon residents have grown accustomed to visitors studying their historic buildings. If you look like you're lost, someone probably will stop to give you directions. That's just part of this town's tradition of hospitality.

Contributor: Eric Minton.

TRAVEL GUIDE

LOCATION—Southwest Ohio, about 20 miles northeast of Cincinnati.

LODGINGS—Standard motels available. Some alternatives: The Artist's Cottage, an 1864 cottage near downtown (doubles $85, 513/932-5938). The Golden Lamb, a hotel landmark with 18 rooms (doubles from $75, 513/932-5065) and restaurant *(see Dining and Food)*. White Tor, a bed and breakfast in a Colonial farmhouse minutes from downtown (doubles from $75, 513/932-5892).

CAMPING—Cedarbrook Campground near downtown (513/932-7717).

DINING AND FOOD—Best Cafe, casual restaurant serving inventive salads (513/932-4400). The Golden Lamb, classic fare in four dining rooms (513/932-5065). Golden Turtle Chocolate Factory, a pure chocolate lover's delight (513/932-1990). Village Ice Cream Parlor, an old-fashioned soda shop (513/932-6918).

SHOPPING—Signs of Our Times, movie and TV memorabilia (513/932-4435).

Turtle Creek Gallery, local and regional artists' works (513/932-2296). Typetiques, Inc., printer's cases and type pieces (513/932-5020).

IN THE AREA—Fort Ancient State Memorial (5 miles northeast of town) is the site of 2,000-year-old Hopewell mounds with hiking trails and picnic spots. Waynesville (10 miles northeast of Lebanon) is an antiquers' paradise with more than 40 shops, as well as stores selling gifts and other specialty items. The Hammel House, a 19th-century stagecoach stop transformed into a restaurant, draws diners from miles around (513/897-2333).

CELEBRATIONS—Old-Fashioned Days in late July. Applefest, in late September. Historic Lebanon Christmas Festival, including a candlelight horse-drawn carriage parade, the first Saturday in December.

INFORMATION—*Warren County Convention & Visitors Bureau, 1073 Oregonia Rd., Ste. A, Lebanon, OH 45036 (800/791-4386).* ■

MORE GREAT TOWNS

Canal villages, college towns and riverside settlements star among Ohio's enticing communities.

Burton

At the center of Burton, a town of 1,349, prim 19th-century buildings in Greek Revival and Victorian-era styles surround the commons, a maple-shaded park. In early spring, the community taps the trees for syrup you can buy in the log cabin on the commons.

Shops around the commons sell country-style home accessories and collectibles, including baskets, quilts and wooden toys. Just off the square, Century Village, 20 historic structures on a hilltop, re-creates an early northeast Ohio town. You can visit homes, a general store, old-time shops, a church and a 1798 log cabin, one of the area's oldest buildings.

Location—Northeast Ohio, 35 miles east of Cleveland.

Information—Geauga County Tourism Council, 8228 Mayfield Rd., Chesterland, OH 44026 (800/775-TOUR).

Coshocton

At the confluence of three rivers, Coshocton (population: 12,200) boomed when the Ohio-Erie Canal opened in 1833. Trains eventually replaced the canal boats. But Roscoe Village, a living-history community just north of town, recaptures the canal days with Greek Revival storefronts, brick sidewalks and wrought-iron lampposts.

Miniature dioramas depicting canal construction fill the Visitors Center Exhibit Hall. Nearby, you can board the *Monticello III,* a horse-drawn canal boat that travels the original waterway.

Visitors flock to the village's restaurants and shops along Whitewoman Street. Costumed "citizens" labor in the shops and homes.

Be sure to stop for ice cream treats at Captain Nye's Coffee and Sweet Shop. You can choose an elegantly furnished room at Roscoe Village Inn or one of the area's several bed and breakfasts.

Fruit simmers at the fall Apple Butter Festival in Burton.

AL TEUFEN

In Yellow Springs, trees engulf residential neighborhoods.

TONY WALSH

Location—North-central Ohio, 65 miles northeast of Columbus.

Information—Coshocton County Convention & Visitors Bureau, Box 905, Coshocton, OH 43812 (800/ 338-4724).

Grand Rapids

The century-old canal town of Grand Rapids (population: 955) follows the banks of the Maumee River in northwest Ohio. Along Front Street, restored buildings brim with antiques and crafts. You'll discover hand-dipped chocolates at a country store and confections at an old-time ice cream shop. The Mill House, once a mill, has been renovated as a bed and breakfast.

Nearby, you can board a replica of an old-time boat for a ride on the Miami-Erie Canal. The *Bluebird* train departs from the Grand Rapids depot for round-trip excursions through farm country to the town of Waterville (10 miles northeast). There, the Columbian House, a restored 1828 inn, serves specialties such as baked ham.

Location—Northwest Ohio, about 25 miles southwest of Toledo.

Information—Grand Rapids Area Chamber of Commerce, Box 391, Grand Rapids, OH 43522 (419/ 832-1106).

Marietta

In a delta where the Muskingum River meets the Ohio, Marietta became the first organized town in the wild Northwest Territory in 1788. Antiques stores and graceful Federal-style homes and museums line the streets of this southeast Ohio River community of 15,000. Hop aboard the trolley, which travels along the river and past gracious homes. The Levee House Cafe, where the pasta is always a favorite, overlooks the Ohio.

At the tip of the delta, visitors can choose the restored Lafayette Hotel, named for the Revolutionary War hero who stayed here in the 1800s. From the hotel, stroll to the Showboat Becky Thatcher Theater and Restaurant. Before the curtain goes up, you can hunt for antiques in historic Hamar Village.

Location—Southeast Ohio, about 125 miles east of Columbus.

Information—Marietta Tourist Con-

vention Bureau, 316 Third St., Marietta, OH 45750 (800/288-2577).

Medina

Connecticut natives who laid out Medina in 1818 designated a commons at the center of town (population: 223,386). Today, that square is an oasis for surrounding businesses. Around the square, shops sell everything from artwork to teddy bears. Mud Mothers Pottery showcases hand-thrown crocks. Ormandy's stocks vintage toy trains. The Medina County Historical Society in an 1886 Victorian home features that era's furnishings and early settlers' heirlooms. Stop in the museum gift shop.

Since 1865, Medina has been the home of candle manufacturer A.I. Root Company. West Liberty Commons, the original Root factory, now houses shops that sell Root products. Grand Market Cafe, a casual restaurant on the historic town square, makes a good dining stop.

Location—Northern Ohio, 35 miles south of Cleveland.

Information—Medina County Convention & Visitors Bureau, 124 W. Lafayette Rd., Suite 100, Medina, OH 44256 (216/722-5502).

Oberlin

Since 1833, this distinguished town of 8,600 and its namesake Oberlin College have grown up around a commons called Tappan Square. Oberlin resembles a tidy New England town. Visitors marvel at the 19th-century First Church, the original meeting house, and the white marble Hall Auditorium, which locals call "Moby Dick." You can browse for gifts at specialty shops.

Most visitors stop in at Gibson's, renowned for plate-sized cinnamon rolls and other delicious baked goods. The Main Street Mercantile Store and Tea Room serves from-scratch soups, salads and inventive pastas. The Ivy Tree Bed and Breakfast, a restored Victorian home, warmly welcomes overnight guests.

Location—Northern Ohio, 30 miles southwest of Cleveland.

Information—Oberlin Area Chamber of Commerce, 20 E. College St., Oberlin, OH 44074 (800/9-OBERLIN).

Put-in-Bay

Islands dot northwest Ohio's Lake Erie shore. By jet ferry from Port Clinton, you're just 25 minutes from South Bass, the largest island, and the town of Put-in-Bay (population: 425).

In summer, vacationers pack the narrow streets, drifting in and out of restaurants and shops. The Beer Barrel Saloon boasts the world's longest bar. Settle in at The Boardwalk restaurant for seafood and a harbor view. A room at the Perry Holiday Island Hotel puts you in the middle of the hubbub.

You can leave crowds behind, strolling pebble-strewn beaches between plunges in the surf. East of town, the 352-foot-high Perry's Victory and International Peace Memorial towers above the harbor, commemorating a pivotal victory in the War of 1812.

Location—Off the Lake Erie shore, about 35 miles east of Toledo.

Information—Put-in-Bay Chamber of Commerce, Box 250, South Bass Island, Put-in-Bay, OH 43456 (419/285-2832).

Yellow Springs

A shady, green oasis not far from the banks of the Little Miami River, Yellow Springs thrives as a free-spirited college town of about 4,000 with an appreciation of its past.

Visitors once flocked to this community, founded in the 1820s, for its mineral springs. You still can reach the springs' source by hiking the Little Miami Scenic Trail to Glen Helen, the 1,000-acre nature preserve that Yellow Springs' Antioch College owns.

Campus buildings rise at the town's east edge. Morgan House Bed and Breakfast, a 1921 Greek Revival structure, was built for Antioch's president. Handsome brick homes line Dayton, Limestone and Phillips streets.

Shopping is best along Xenia and Dayton streets. Browse Victorian storefronts for pottery, stained glass, jewelry and books. Stop at Winds Cafe for dining in a gallery setting or Carol's Kitchen for salads and sandwiches.

Location—Southwest Ohio, 20 miles northeast of Dayton.

Information—Chamber of Commerce, 108 Dayton St., Yellow Springs, OH 45387 (937/767-2686). ■

WISCONSIN

BARABOO • BAYFIELD • CAMBRIDGE CEDARBURG • FISH CREEK • HUDSON MINERAL POINT • NEW GLARUS PORT WASHINGTON

Wisconsin stands out as a state tailor-made for small-town touring. Varied landscapes—from rugged lakeshore up north to hills and green pastures of dairy country to the south—add special pleasure. You'll explore resilient towns that bounced back from tough times, genteel communities that are centers for artists and crafters, and towns that take great pride in their ethnic heritage. What's more, local residents are almost certain to be having as much fun as you will when you visit.

For information about additional Wisconsin small towns you can visit, contact: *Wisconsin Dept. of Tourism, Box 7976, Madison, WI 53707-7976 (800/432-8747).*

CEDARBURG

Preservationists sparked a turnaround in this town with a thriving arts-and-crafts community.

The German stonemasons who built Cedarburg would be proud. In this Currier and Ives community 20 minutes north of Milwaukee, square-shouldered structures of limestone and cream-colored brick line up along the main streets as solidly as they have for more than a century. The spires of imposing churches tower above the rooftops, and two historic mills still rise along serene Cedar Creek.

Today, many of the old storefronts and former homes have become shops, selling everything from antiques to locally made wine and fine jewelry. In studios and workshops, you'll discover the creations of weavers, potters, teddy-bear artists and metalsmiths. More than 50 artisans live and work here, carrying on a tradition of fine craftsmanship that began with the hardworking builders of the town.

The Downtown Revival
In the mid-1800s, five mills hummed along the banks of Cedar Creek. The mills drew workers and spurred the creation of many other businesses. Cedarburg prospered. But by the 1970s, the town, like many small Midwest communities, was struggling for survival. Cedarburg's biggest asset was its abundance of old buildings that had survived, as if waiting for just the right time to be rediscovered.

Former Mayor Stephen Fischer urged the City Council to reject a plan to bulldoze one of the old mills to make way for a gas station. Jim and Sandy Pape bought the musty old mill building and sparked a turnaround.

"This place was considered a white elephant," Sandy recalls with a smile. "No one wanted it."

Today, the mill and two adjacent restored buildings, known as Cedar Creek Settlement, form the centerpiece of the revitalized downtown. The complex comprises a winery and more than two dozen artists' studios, restaurants, gift shops and antiques dealers.

In the settlement's main building, visitors can tour the cool stone cellars of the Cedar Creek Winery, where vintages age in 55-gallon oak casks. Take the tour or just stop in to sample some of Cedar Creek's 10 varieties. Try the popular cranberry blush or the award-winning Cedar Creek Vidal.

Ken and Kay Walters bought a turn-of-the-century limestone building and transformed it into the Cedarburg Woolen Mill. There, you can watch an 1860s wool-carding machine at work. The shop sells spinning, quilting and weaving supplies, as well as rag rugs and custom-made quilts.

Antiquers' Haven
The preservationist spirit spread along Washington Avenue, the main thoroughfare, to surrounding downtown streets. Historic buildings now shelter about 100 shops and restaurants.

An old stone brewery has been transformed into an art center. Make an appointment to tour The Kuhefuss House, an 1849 Greek Revival home.

A five-story gristmill that towers beside Cedar Creek was another candidate for the wrecking ball. Instead, it houses a feed store that caters to bird lovers with more than 500 backyard feeders. To the delight of Cedarburg's preservationists, you can walk through part of the building that remains much as it was when the mill ground grain.

Antiques shops attract collectors, browsers and history buffs. Spool 'n Spindle, a cooperative of 10 dealers in Cedar Creek Settlement, stocks all sorts of antique furniture and collectibles dating from 1850s through the Depression era. Dime A Dance sells vintage clothing and lace.

Eight stores have taken over the former city hall, now known as the Washington Avenue Shoppes Mall. Browsers survey pottery, toys, folk art and local artists' works.

At the center of downtown, the exterior of the Washington House Inn appears much as it did during the late 1800s. At that time, the establishment

This renovated mill houses shops, plus artists' and crafters' studios.

provided rooms for salesmen and other travelers who came to do business in the thriving mill town. Inside, the 34 restored rooms pamper guests with antique furnishings, fireplaces and whirlpool baths.

Downtown, The Stagecoach Inn Bed and Breakfast, an 1853 Greek Revival stone building, once was a way station for travelers on the road from Green Bay to Milwaukee. Now, guests settle into 12 antique-filled rooms.

Artful Eateries

More than a dozen restaurants, from casual coffeehouses to more elegant special-occasion eateries, cater to a variety of tastes. Barth's at the Bridge, a showcase for artwork and antiques, features authentic German dishes on the menu, along with juicy prime rib. After 50 years, the restaurant ranks as a Cedarburg institution.

The Settlers Inn occupies a restored 1846 tavern that still has its original bar. Owners Tom and Joan Dorsey proudly serve from-scratch soups and jumbo muffins. (Regulars usually favor the cranberry-almond and chocolate chip-banana.) For lunch, order a deli sandwich and save room for a wedge of from-scratch pie.

At Morton's, a friendly pub, almost everyone orders two-fisted burgers. Choosing a beer from the list of 75 takes more thought.

Quilts decorate weathered stone walls, and diners use antique flatware at the Cream and Crepe Cafe in Cedar Creek Settlement. Entrée crepes take the names of quilt patterns. Regular diners rave about the "combination star," a ham-asparagus-and-Swiss-cheese creation.

For dessert, sample the crepe wrapped around soft vanilla ice cream and topped with caramel, hot fudge and nuts. "Once people try it," owner Donna Taylor says, "they have to have it every time they eat here."

Crafters at Work

The town's thriving community of artists and crafters has grown steadily over the last two decades. Galleries with tall windows and rough walls of brick and stone provide settings for a range of creations.

Weavers, two photographers, a watercolorist and children's author

Grape-stomping is part of the fun at the Wine and Harvest Festival.

JOHN M. TOUSCANY/THIRD COAST

Barbara Joosse occupy space on the second floor of the Cedarburg Woolen Mill downtown. You can watch the artists at work and buy their finished pieces. In the old brewery, the Ozaukee Art Center displays striking sculptures. Metalsmiths Mike and Beth Eubanks create pieces in gold and sterling silver at The Jewelry Works.

Dave and Pat Eitel numbered among the first artists who decided to set up shop at Cedar Creek Settlement. Today, their pottery studio looks out on Cedarburg's old mill pond through the wavy panes of the mill's original glass. When Dave and Pat were searching for a new studio location almost two decades ago, they discovered the old woolen mill almost by accident.

The gallery showcases the Eitels' sturdy stoneware crocks, along with other local artists' works. The sunny space displays handcrafted ceramic tiles, stained glass, jewelry and whimsically painted candleholders.

Dave helped found the Cedarburg Artists Guild, which puts on shows each year during Cedarburg's acclaimed winter festival.

The same friendly, small-town serenity and sense of the past that attracted crafters and artists to the village of Cedarburg combine to draw visitors here today.

"Cedar Creek Settlement was the anchor," Dave explains proudly. "But now, people come to see the whole town."
By Diana McMillen.

TRAVEL GUIDE

LOCATION—Eastern Wisconsin, 20 miles north of Milwaukee.

LODGINGS—Standard motels cluster nearby along I-43. Some alternatives: The Stagecoach Inn, a 12-room bed and breakfast in a building constructed in 1853 (doubles from $70, 888/375-0208). The Washington House Inn, a bed and breakfast in a historic hotel (doubles from $69, 800/554-4717).

DINING AND FOOD—Amy's Candy Kitchen for fine chocolates (800/513-8889). Barth's at the Bridge, prime rib and authentic German foods (414/377-0660). Cedar Creek Winery, tours and samples of local wines (800/827-8020). Chocolate Factory, old-fashioned ice cream parlor and sandwich shop (414/377-8877). Cream and Crepe Cafe in Cedar Creek Settlement (414/377-0900). Settlers Inn for home-style muffins, pies and inventive sandwiches in a historic tavern (414/377-4466). Morton's for burgers and beer (414/377-4779).

SHOPPING—B.J. Beck's Toys, creative playthings from around the world in an 1880 building. Button Nook, one of the largest collections of antique buttons in the country, operated by

B.J. Beck's owner, Bruce Beck (open by appointment, 414/375-3001). Cedar Creek Pottery, crocks and other local artists' works (414/375-1226). Cedarburg Woolen Mill for clothes, quilts, and sewing and weaving supplies, and Cedarburg Woolen Mill Studios (414/377-0345). Dime A Dance, vintage clothes, linens and more (414/377-5054). Jewelry Works, handcrafted pieces in a range of prices (414/377-9010). Marline's General Store for candles, pottery and handcrafted furnishings (414/375-5040).

IN THE AREA—Walk across the only remaining covered bridge in Wisconsin at Covered Bridge Park (1 mile north of Cedarburg). You can picnic along the banks of Cedar Creek. Also visit the tiny town of Hamilton (1 mile southeast). This 130-year-old village, with its stone homes and mill, is a state historic site.

CELEBRATIONS—Strawberry & Jazz Festival in June. Wine and Harvest Festival in September. Christmas in the Country in early December.

INFORMATION—*Cedarburg Chamber of Commerce, W63 N645, Washington Ave., Box 104, Cedarburg, WI 53012 (800/CDR-BURG).* ■

FISH CREEK

This town enchants visitors at the heart of one of Wisconsin's most popular vacation playgrounds.

Lake Michigan breezes cool the solitary, rocky shore on the quieter east side of the Door County Peninsula. This 70-mile-long finger of land has been one of Wisconsin's favorite vacation areas for more than a century. Along Green Bay on the peninsula's western shore, 1900s-era fishing villages have grown into bustling enclaves of shops, inns, cottage colonies and restaurants.

The village of Fish Creek, though never formerly incorporated as a town, is one of the best places to sample Door County attractions. It's not far from the peninsula's tip on the Green Bay side. The streets fill up with cars on summer weekends, but no matter. You can manage most of the village (population: 300) easily on foot, and strolling is almost an official pastime.

Beside the Bay

As you drive the twisting descent from Clark Bluff, Fish Creek unfolds like a picture-book New England harbor town. Whitewashed clapboard shops and inns line up along sun-dappled Main Street. Sloops sway in the harbor, and the massive limestone bluff of Peninsula State Park rises to the east. The placid waters of Green Bay spread before you, along with other scalloped bays and arcs of sand.

Start your tour along Main Street (State-42), where maples arch overhead, and cheery petunias and impatiens line the walks in summer. You'll find plenty to explore along this corridor, which stretches less than a mile from bayfront Sunset Park east toward the entrance to Peninsula State Park.

North of Main Street, cottages and other lodgings fill the few blocks to the curving waterfront and Fish Creek's busy marina. To the south, Cottage Row winds lazily along the shore, offering glimpses of some of the county's most extravagant summer homes.

Shops in Fish Creek seem to outnumber full-time residents, and the selection grows almost daily. Even an old gas station now houses the Olde Station Shops, selling fancy sweatshirts, pizza and frozen yogurt. A former ice cream shop has become the Hide Side Boutique, featuring hand-painted women's clothes.

A few Fish Creek institutions remain, too, such as the delightfully dark and musty Fish Creek General Store and adjacent Alwes Food Market. They've occupied the corner of Main and Spruce streets since the town's early, quieter days.

One of the most popular shopping draws is Founder's Square along Main Street. A dozen or so shops occupy original and reconstructed settlers' buildings, scattered along a shady cedar-bark path.

At the Stone Cutter lapidary shop, you'll get a combination geology and history lesson. Featuring stones from across the globe, the shop tucks into a creaking, slightly listing cabin. It's the original homestead of one of Fish Creek's founders, Asa Thorp.

A Century of Popularity

Fish Creek was a budding steamer stop and fishing village when Thorp arrived in the mid-1800s. By the turn of the century, the community had become a popular vacation spot, with an inn and casino drawing steamship travelers from southern Lake Michigan. Today, those neighboring buildings still cater to travelers as the White Gull and Whistling Swan inns.

It's just two short blocks from the Whistling Swan to quiet Clark Park, a shady expanse of lawn overlooking the waterfront. You can rent paddleboats and sailboats there or simply relax to the rhythmic clang of sailboat halyards.

Charter-boat operations offer fishing trips and cruises among the Chamber Islands and other islands that sprinkle across Green Bay. For landlubbers, historical walking tours depart daily from the old Gibraltar Town Hall, located across Spruce Street.

DARRYL R. BEERS

Green Bay
sunsets paint the
sky at Fish Creek.

State Park Exploring

Just north of Fish Creek, Peninsula State Park stands out as a star Door County attraction. At this enormous 3,700-acre preserve that juts into Green Bay, you can indulge in a host of outdoor activities. Fine beachside camping and beachcombing, plus bicycling, golfing and hiking number among the park's favored pastimes.

The 5-mile gravel Sunset Cycling Trail dips among birches and pines along the shores of tranquil Tennison Bay. You may surprise a shy fawn or an industrious beaver.

Mountain bikers enjoy the trails' newest addition: 8 miles of dirt and gravel paths that travel deep into the park's interior (trail pass required). You can rent sturdy mountain bikes just outside the park entrance.

Golfers should plan well ahead to play the acclaimed 18-hole Peninsula State Park golf course. Its rolling fairways overlook Eagle Harbor. Book a tee time in writing after January 1 (75-cent reservation charge per person: Box 218, Fish Creek, WI 54212). You also can make reservations by phone a week or less in advance of your visit (414/854-5791).

Be sure to take time to climb the park's observation tower. A view of the half-dozen islands rising just offshore spreads before you.

The adjacent Eagle Trail traces a steep and rocky route between the bluff and lake below. Visitors can tour the 1868 lighthouse at Eagle Bluff for another fine view. Climb partway up the tower and peer out across the lake and shore that this light, now solar powered, still overlooks.

"Door County has more lighthouses—a total of nine—than any other county in the U.S.," guide Grace Adams explains during her fact-packed 30-minute tour.

Fish Boils And Other Fare

The Door County Peninsula's food traditions revolve around the lake's bounty and the area's abundant cherry orchards. You'll see them almost everywhere. Be sure to make reservations well in advance for a fish boil at Fish Creek's White Gull Inn or nearby Pelletier's restaurant. This renowned fisherman's feast of boiled whitefish, onions, red potatoes, cole slaw, bread and Door County cherry pie is part meal and part event.

Grab a beverage and a spot on the patio to witness the drama when cooks splash kerosene over an open flame

Just south of Fish Creek, you can visit Lautenbach's Orchard Country.

DARRYL R. BEERS

roaring beneath a huge kettle. A brilliant fireball blazes up to heat the kettle, which boils over, removing fishy oils from the pot.

But don't overlook other dining options throughout Fish Creek. At The Cookery, warm sunlight pours through the big bay windows while guests savor chunky cherry applesauce, steaming crocks of whitefish chowder and other dishes that have a distinct Door County flair.

Carol Skare creates many of the restaurant's recipes. Along with her husband, Dick, Carol owns and operates the popular eatery along Main Street. The Skares discovered Door County on their honeymoon about 20 years ago and opened The Cookery later that year.

"Of course, we've just fallen in love with the area," Carol says without reservation. "Being around the water and this beautiful countryside is just a dream come true."

By Tina Lassen.

TRAVEL GUIDE

LOCATION—Northeast Wisconsin, 180 miles north of Milwaukee.

LODGINGS—Thousands of rooms available, from the simple to the luxurious (reservations recommended). For lodging availability, contact the Door County Chamber of Commerce (see Information). Some favorites in Fish Creek: Apple Creek Resort, one- and two-room motel suites, indoor pool and whirlpool near Peninsula State Park (doubles from $89, ask about packages, 800/569-0059). Harbor Guest House along the lakefront, seven one- and two-bedroom apartments with full kitchens, pool and tennis courts (one-bedroom units from $158, 920/868-2284). Main Street Motel, individually decorated motel units in the heart of town (doubles from $79, 920/868-2201). The Whistling Swan, a century-old inn near shopping and restaurants (doubles from $99, including breakfast, 920/868-3442).

CAMPING—Peninsula State Park, four campgrounds, some with hookups. Reservations at the park office or by mail only: Box 218, Fish Creek, WI 54212.

DINING AND FOOD—The Black Locust, classic, elegant fare (920/868-2999). The Cookery, inventive dishes with local fruits and flavors such as pork tenderloin with cherry chutney (920/868-3634). White Gull Inn, fish boil, as well as one of the peninsula's best breakfasts, including homemade granola and cherry-stuffed French toast (920/868-3517).

SHOPPING—At Founder's Square along Main Street, Wilkins and Olander for classic sportswear (920/868-3168). J. Jeffrey Taylor, fine arts and custom jewelers (920/868-3033). Sunshine and Company, birdbaths, wind chimes and almost everything else for your yard (920/868-3202). In Sister Bay, Jack Anderson Gallery for originals and prints by one of the county's best-known artists (920/854-5161).

IN THE AREA—The Peninsula Players Summer Theater, the nation's oldest professional resident summer stock company, brings Broadway and off-Broadway shows outdoors to the shores of Green Bay every night except Mondays (920/868-3287). The theater is located along State-42 just south of Fish Creek. Birch Creek Music Center presents acclaimed concerts by its students all summer in a renovated barn east of Egg Harbor (5 miles south of Fish Creek, 920/868-3763).

CELEBRATIONS— Peninsula Music Festival several weeks every August. Winter Games in February.

INFORMATION—Door County Chamber of Commerce, Box 406, Sturgeon Bay, WI 54235 (920/743-4456). ■

MINERAL POINT

Cornish immigrants helped this town boom. Now, it's known for its thriving artists' colony.

A late-afternoon breeze ripples through Frank Polizzi's pottery workshop and studio. His feet rhythmically pushing the pedals that drive the round stone of his potter's wheel, Frank hunches over 3 pounds of brown clay. With speed and grace, the clay rises to form a delicately curving water pitcher.

"This craft has changed little in centuries," Frank explains, as onlookers pepper him with questions. "It's as old as these hills and as rewarding as each new sunrise."

The potter's poetic description of his art nearly perfectly characterizes the town where he practices it. Mineral Point, a onetime Cornish mining town and today a mecca for artists, crafters and history buffs, appears as old as southwest Wisconsin's surrounding limestone hills. The historic buildings bring a time-honored beauty to this community of 2,428 residents, and the artists who work here add an inviting whimsical atmosphere.

Crafters' Treasures

Galleries and artists' workshops occupy sturdy brick and limestone storefronts, most more than a century old. They crowd High Street, Mineral Point's main thoroughfare, and the surrounding steep, winding streets of the business district. Modest honey-colored miners' cottages, with stone walls 2 feet thick, share surrounding shady residential avenues. The streets are lined with lavish Victorian mansions that 19th-century mining magnates and wealthy merchants built.

From its second-floor perch on a building that now houses a delicatessen, Mineral Point's best-loved pet, a zinc statue of a noble hound, has watched the traffic on High Street for more than 110 years. The dog gained fame as the symbol of Gundry and Gray, once southwest Wisconsin's most elegant department store.

High Street meanders eastward until it bumps into Commerce, another Mineral Point thoroughfare. Commerce teems with shops, antiques stores and more pottery studios. Additional stores crowd Jail Alley, named for a long-gone lockup. The sign on the door of one gallery that's closed for the afternoon captures Mineral Point's laid-back attitude: "Please come up to the stone house with the green shutters. Knock! If I'm home, I'll reopen."

Like many of the town's artists and crafters, Bert and Jean Bohlin fell in love with Mineral Point as visitors before they retired here and opened Needlewood along Jail Alley in an 1847 brick-and-limestone home. The shop sells handmade furniture, needlepoint, quilts and finely crafted wood sculptures.

Where Wisconsin Began

Artists started arriving in Mineral Point in the 1930s. But the town traces its roots to at least 1827, when lead in the surrounding hills attracted miners from across the Midwest. Mining reigned as the undisputed king of industry here for more than 100 years.

The influx of settlers prompted the federal government to establish the Wisconsin Territory, and Mineral Point became its most important city. Colonel Henry Dodge took his oath of office as the territory's first governor under the big shade tree that still spreads its branches over Library Park downtown. The library next door houses an extensive collection of early maps, newspapers and photographs.

News of the lead boom soon reached England and, by the 1830s, hard-rock miners from Cornwall arrived in Mineral Point. With their skills, they went deeper into the limestone hills for lead and copper than the locals, whom the Cornish derisively called "badgers."

The Cornish immigrants also brought a talent for stonemasonry. Many of them built sturdy stone cottages beside the mines along Shake Rag Street, just north of downtown.

In the early 1970s, Mineral Point's

last working mine limped toward closure. At the same time, the arts-and-crafts community started to bloom, and preservationists started working to restore and recognize significant buildings. The historic district, with more than 900 buildings, became the first in Wisconsin listed in the National Register of Historic Places.

Cornish Roots Remain

Pendarvis House, preserved as a state historic site, celebrates Mineral Point's Cornish heritage. Guides costumed in the 1800s dress of Cornish settlers walk visitors through 10 buildings along Shake Rag Street, including several 1830s stone cottages, a row house and Cornish pub.

From across Shake Rag Street, a trail winds around the Merry Christmas Mine, where the zinc played out near the turn of the century.

How did the street acquire the name Shake Rag? Most of the miners lived across the street from the mines. On working days, miners' wives would shake rags at their husbands from cottage windows to alert them that lunch was on the table.

Hearty Cornish fare, including pasties (pronounced PASS-tees), often starred at those midday meals. Today, you can sample the thick, stewlike meat-potato-and-vegetable creations baked inside a sturdy crust, at the Red Rooster Cafe and the Royal Inn, both along High Street downtown.

Local restaurants also serve other Cornish specialties such as Mawgan meatballs, saffron cake, tea biscuits and figgyhobbin, a dessert pastry rolled in raisins and often served with warm caramel sauce.

Driving Tour

Each new discovery brought more wealth to local mine owners, merchants and lawyers. Many embarked on building binges and constructed the elaborate Victorian homes that line Ridge Street and grace surrounding neighborhoods. A driving-tour guide, which you can pick up at the visitors

Sturdy, limestone-and-brick structures line Main Street.

JON WEISS

Cornish cottages remind visitors of Mineral Point's beginnings.

Swiss immigrants founded the town in 1845, and newcomers have been arriving from the mother country ever since.

In the two-block business district, ordinary buildings mingle with fanciful Swiss structures. Visitors browse downtown and sample Swiss fare at local restaurants. Shops stock sausages, wood carvings, and imports from chocolate to music boxes. Saturdays (May–November), you can tour New Glarus Brewing Company.

At the New Glarus Hotel or Glarner Stube restaurant, you can sample Wiener schnitzel. Stop in Ruef's Meat Market for from-scratch sausages. The Chalet Landhaus Inn resembles a low-slung Swiss chalet.

Location—*South-central Wisconsin, 30 miles south of Madison.*

Information—*New Glarus Tourism, Box 713, New Glarus, WI 53574-0713 (800/527-6838).*

Port Washington

Wheeling gulls and clanging sailboat halyards mark your arrival in Port Washington, a town of 10,000 along the central Lake Michigan shore. Water defines this town, one of the Great Lakes' prime sport-fishing ports.

Streets plunge down steep hills to the wide harbor. St. Mary's Church, a Gothic masterpiece, crowns one of the highest hills. The church almost seems to be standing guard over downtown and the harbor.

Sample the day's catch at the well-known Smith Bros. Fish Shanty. Parrots Landing specializes in casual outdoor dining with a marina view.

You can browse a half-dozen shops in the business district. At Wind in the Rigging, you'll discover nautical glassware and clothing, along with no-nonsense boating equipment. Holiday decorations crowd Christmas in Port.

You'll pass anglers along the breakwater en route to the Art Deco lighthouse that stands over the marina. For a lake view, try the Best Western Harborside Motor Inn. For turn-of-the-century atmosphere, stay at the Grand Inn or Inn at Old Twelve Hundred.

Location—*Central Wisconsin's Lake Michigan shore, about 25 miles north of Milwaukee.*

Information—*Port Washington Tourism Office, 126 E. Grand Ave., Port Washington, WI 53074 (414/ 284-0900).* ■

St. Mary's Church, a landmark in Port Washington.

For lodging and dining, try the Old Rittenhouse Inn in Bayfield.

PETER LINDMAN

spoiled Apostle Islands archipelago. A car ferry also shuttles visitors to Madeline Island. Sightseeing cruises and kayak tours explore smaller islands.

Location—Northwest Wisconsin, 75 miles east of Duluth, Minnesota.

Information—Bayfield Chamber of Commerce, 42 S. Broad St., Box 138, Bayfield, WI 54814 (800/447-4094).

Cambridge

Along the shores of Lake Ripley in south-central Wisconsin, this community of 1,000 residents grew up as a resort town and farming center. Today, Cambridge proudly calls itself the "Salt-Glazed Pottery Capital of the World."

Crafters at Rowe Pottery Works along Main Street (State-12) make stoneware and wrought-iron pieces using old-time methods. Crocks, plates and other creations fill the showroom.

Antiques dealers and an old-fashioned bakery that sells memorable cream puffs number among more than two dozen shops in early 1900s storefronts downtown. Specialty shops occupy a renovated wagon factory. One sells Victorian-inspired accessories; another puts together gift baskets of made-in-Wisconsin products.

Location—South-central Wisconsin, about 20 miles southeast of Madison.

Information—Cambridge Chamber of Commerce, 102 Main St., Box 330, Cambridge, WI 53523 (608/423-3780).

Hudson

Because the St. Croix River Valley reminded 19th-century settlers of scenery back east in New York state, they named their new community after the Hudson River Valley. The town of Hudson, with 6,400 residents, grew up around sawmills during the valley's logging boom.

Lumbermen and merchants built some of the sturdy brick buildings you still see in the business district. It's an enclave of specialty shops that rises between the river and inland bluffs.

After the boom faded, the town settled into a relaxed pace that hasn't change much in generations. During summer, pleasure craft ply the river, and Hudson's population swells with boaters and vacationers.

Innkeepers have transformed a number of the grand old homes into bed and breakfasts such as the Jefferson-Day House and opulent Phipps Inn. You can tour the Octagon House, an architectural curiosity that's home to the local historical society.

Location—West-central Wisconsin, about 15 miles east of Minnesota's Twin Cities.

Information—Hudson Chamber of Commerce & Tourism Bureau, 502 Second St., Box 438, Hudson, WI 54016-0438 (800/657-6775).

New Glarus

This community of about 1,900 calls itself "America's Little Switzerland."

MORE GREAT TOWNS

These towns span the state, from "Little Switzerland" in the south to Bayfield Peninsula up north.

Baraboo

Ringling Brothers Circus was born in Baraboo, and the legendary troupe once made this south-central Wisconsin town of 9,800 its winter home.

Shops and cafes, many in vintage buildings constructed with Ringling wealth, surround the courthouse square. Movies still play at the Al Ringling Theater, as fanciful as a circus wagon. Curlicues and stone carvings decorate the facade.

Turn-of-the-century homes with gingerbread trim line neighboring streets. The architecture of many of the houses reminds you of the flamboyance of the circus performers.

Wander among the ornate circus wagons, colorful posters and glittering costumes in the Circus World Museum along Water Street. In the summer, acclaimed circus acts perform under a big top on the museum grounds.

Location—South-central Wisconsin, about 30 miles north of Madison.

Information—Baraboo Area Chamber of Commerce, 124 Second St., Baraboo, WI 53913 (608/356-8333).

Bayfield

This once-booming logging and fishing town now counts fewer than 700 residents. It overlooks Apostle Islands National Lakeshore from a hilly peninsula that rolls down to northern Wisconsin's Lake Superior shore.

A walking tour takes you to more than 50 buildings listed in the National Register of Historic Places, including imposing Victorian beauties that have become bed and breakfasts. The Old Rittenhouse Inn is known for its cozy, antique-furnished rooms, memorable food and warm hospitality.

Boutiques and specialty shops in the half-dozen blocks downtown showcase the works of a thriving artists' community. Restaurants such as Pier Plaza and Greunke's serve steaks, fresh whitefish and other hearty fare.

Sailboats leave the busy little harbor, bound for Madeline Island and the un-

Kids of all ages delight in the Circus World Museum in Baraboo.

JOHN NIENHUIS

bureau, pinpoints opulent homes and other historic sites.

Dry goods merchants Joseph Gundry and John Gray each commissioned an enormous mansion. Gundry called his 11-acre estate on Madison Street Orchard Lawn. You can tour the lavish Italianate home, built in 1868, and gardens, preserved as the Mineral Point Historical Society's museum.

In 1906, William A. Jones, the U.S. Commissioner of Indian Affairs under President McKinley, built a mansion along Ridge Street befitting his position. When Jones died shortly thereafter, the house stood shuttered for nearly 75 years. Now restored, the mansion retains its original library, carpets, many antique furnishings and all of its turn-of-the-century elegance.

The Cothren House along Tower Street, now also a bed and breakfast, displays the craftsmanship of Mineral Point's Cornish stonemasons. Built in 1853, this two-story renovated estate features 2-foot-thick walls, an airy summer kitchen, spacious formal gardens and a restored log cabin.

When you visit, beware of Mineral Point's charm. Many of the artists and innkeepers first came here as visitors, but this town has a way of turning its guests into permanent residents.

By Alan Guebert.

TRAVEL GUIDE

LOCATION—Southwest Wisconsin, 45 miles southwest of Madison.

LODGINGS—Standard motel rooms available. Some alternatives: The Cothren House, five guest rooms (doubles from $65, 608/987-2612). House of the Brau-meister, a Queen Anne home on historic Shake Rag Street (doubles from $55). Knudson's Guest House, antiques and Amish quilts in three guest rooms (doubles $70, 608/987-2733).

CAMPING—Governor Dodge State Park (10 miles north), second-largest state park in Wisconsin, with 5,000 acres of steep bluffs and quiet valleys. Boating, canoe rentals, horseback riding, mountain-bike trail, hiking and 267 camping sites, some with hookups. Reservations recommended (608/935-3325).

DINING AND FOOD—Red Rooster Cafe, full menu specializing in Cornish fare (608/987-9936). Royal Inn, steaks, fish and Cornish specialties (608/987-3051).

SHOPPING—Against the Grain Wood Works for hardwood sculptures (608/987-2329). The Foundry Books for works on Wisconsin and regional history (608/987-4363). Johnston Gallery, contemporary crafts, art and pottery from 130 artists (608/987-3787). Mulberry Pottery, working studio selling handmade stoneware and porcelain (608/987-2680). Needlewood for Amish quilts, needle art, clocks and wood sculptures (608/987-2813). Old Stand Gallery, watercolors and wood sculptures (608/987-3847). Paper Mountain Books for used books, children's books and toy soldiers (608/987-2320).

IN THE AREA—Dozens of artists and crafters also work in Mount Horeb, a Norwegian settlement about 35 miles east. Nearby at Little Norway, costumed guides lead tours through a pioneer Norwegian homestead transformed into a museum. Information: *Mount Horeb Chamber of Commerce (88-TROLLWAY).*

CELEBRATIONS—Real Antique Show in mid-June. Mineral Point Art Festival downtown in mid-August. Taste of Mineral Point and Annual Cornish Festival downtown in late September. Artisans Guild Christmas Walk, galleries, studios and shops open weekends between Thanksgiving and Christmas.

INFORMATION—*Mineral Point Visitors Bureau, 225 High St., Mineral Point, WI 53565-1209 (888/POINT-WI).* ■